craft workshop

basket

craft workshop

basket

Polly Pollock

photography by Peter Williams

southwater

This edition is published by Southwater

Southwater is an imprint of Anness Publishing Ltd
Hermes House, 88–89 Blackfriars Road, London SE1 8HA
tel. 020 7401 2077; fax 020 7633 9499
www.southwaterbooks.com; info@anness.com

This edition distributed in the UK by The Manning Partnership Ltd, 6 The Old Dairy, Melcombe Road, Bath BA2 3LR; tel. 01225 478 444; fax 01225 478 440; sales@manning-partnership.co.uk

This edition distributed in the USA and Canada by National Book Network, 4720 Boston Way, Lanham, MD 20706; tel. 301 459 3366; fax 301 459 1705; www.nbnbooks.com

This edition distributed in Australia by Pan Macmillan Australia, Level 18, St Martins Tower, 31 Market St, Sydney, NSW 2000; tel. 1300 135 113; fax 1300 135 103; customer.service@macmillan.com.au

This edition distributed in New Zealand by The Five Mile Press (NZ) Ltd, PO Box 33–1071 Takapuna, Unit 11/101–111 Diana Drive, Glenfield, Auckland 10; tel. (09) 444 4144; fax (09) 444 4518; fivemilenz@clear.net.nz

Previously published as *New Crafts: Basketwork*

Publisher: Joanna Lorenz
Senior Editor: Lindsay Porter
Designer: Lilian Lindblom
Photographer: Peter Williams
Stylist: Georgina Rhodes
Illustrators: Madeleine David and Lucinda Ganderton

10 9 8 7 6 5 4 3 2 1

Disclaimer

Learning a new craft is great fun and can fill many rewarding hours, but some tools may need to be handled with care. The author and publishers have made every effort to ensure that all the instructions in this book are accurate and safe, and therefore cannot accept liability for any resulting injury, damage or loss to persons or property, however it may arise.

Contents

Introduction

There can be few households without a basket of some description. Today, many baskets are imported from South-East Asia and Eastern Europe.

This book aims to capture a growing interest in making, instead of simply buying, baskets and introduces the reader to the wonderfully wide array of baskets across the world – their various forms, functions, materials, techniques, colours and patterns. Basketry is a much greater subject than most people imagine, and this book provides an insight into using two of its materials – cane and willow. The historical and gallery sections and the projects will, we hope, inspire readers to find out more about this craft.

The projects are arranged to allow the reader to get the feel of the materials first, then to introduce the techniques necessary for making more ambitious pieces. Have fun adding to the number of baskets in your home!

Left: Many basket-makers working today are still making baskets to traditional designs. The bouirricou (far left), herring cran (centre) and eel trap (left) are such examples.

HISTORY

BASKETRY EVOLVED OUT OF THE NEED TO CONTAIN AND TRANSPORT THINGS. IT IS ARGUABLY THE MOST ANCIENT OF CRAFTS AND ITS MANY DESIGNS HAVE EVOLVED OVER CENTURIES. IT IS PRACTISED VIRTUALLY ALL OVER THE WORLD AND, BEING SO FUNCTIONAL, HAS RESULTED IN VERY SIMILAR DESIGNS OCCURING EVERYWHERE. MANY OF ITS TECHNIQUES HAVE EVOLVED INDEPENDENTLY IN DIFFERENT PARTS OF THE WORLD, REFLECTING MATERIALS READILY AVAILABLE.

Traditionally, basketry materials come directly from nature; they are often gathered from the wild, or as by-products of crops, such as wheat or rice straw, corn husks, or leaves from fruit-bearing palms.

The basket-making industry declined rapidly in developed countries since the Second World War. Vegetables, fruit and fish which used to be transported in baskets (fish and small animals were sometimes trapped in them) now go straight in to other, manufactured types of container – wooden and cardboard boxes and, more recently, plastic containers. Baskets no longer function as official measures: the bushels used in hop and apple picking, pecks for peas and beans and crans for herring have been superseded. Shopping baskets have been more or less displaced by paper or plastic carrier bags.

In recent years, however, there has been a revival of interest in the worldwide craft. Membership of basketry associations and enrolment on basketry courses are increasing, more books are being published and more exhibitions of both traditional and contemporary basketry mounted. The number of both professional and amateur makers is growing, as well as those with a more academic interest in the craft.

There are several reasons for this revival. One is a reaction against the bland, homogenized output of modern industry and the way of life associated with it. This leads to an appreciation of individually crafted objects, and a desire among a growing number of people to make objects

Above: A selection of basketry objects from eastern, central and southern Africa (triangular dish, container with pointed lid, beer skimmers and bracelets) made from straw and grass, and Native American baskets made from cedar root, split poplar and oak.

Left: Storage and carrying baskets made from palm and reeds from southern Africa.

rather than simply to act as consumers. This in turn leads to a wish to be involved in all stages of the process, from gathering or growing basketry materials to weaving them for use or for sale. Another related reason is the emergence of basket-making at the end of the craft-art continuum. Until recently, basketry was rarely used as a medium for creative self expression and although this is still largely the case, there are some exceptions. In the past, most basket-makers were anonymous, while today many can be recognized by their work. A growing number of people are experimenting with new materials and forms. Many are using traditional materials in non-traditional ways, or are using unexpected materials to create strongly individual designs.

While fully acknowledging the beauty of traditional basket-making and the influence it has on their work, these contemporary basket-makers also value the concept and visual impact of their work as much as, if not more than, its practical use.

Right: Basketry objects from South-East Asia, all of which are connected with the preparation and serving of food.

Below: Baskets from west and southern Africa made using a variety of techniques, but all from palm leaves.

Left: Two European baskets. The one on the left is made from split chestnut, and comes from Northern Portugal. On the right is an egg basket from France made of cane.

GALLERY

THE WORK OF MANY OF TODAY'S BASKET-MAKERS IS OFTEN A COMBINATION OF THE TRADITIONAL AND CONTEMPORARY. MANY USE AGE-OLD MATERIALS IN CONTEMPORARY WAYS TO CREATE STRONGLY INDIVIDUAL DESIGNS, OR USE NEWER MATERIALS SUCH AS METAL WIRE TO WEAVE SMALL, INTRICATE PIECES.

Top: GREAT REED MACE
These are made from skeined buff willow, using a spiralling plaiting technique over a core of carved wood, which also forms the leaves and stems.
MARIAN GWIAZDA

Above: OLIVE POD
This piece, made from dyed cane and dyed cotton is made using a "complex-linking" technique. The technique has its origins in the hammocks made in South America.
SHUNA RENDEL

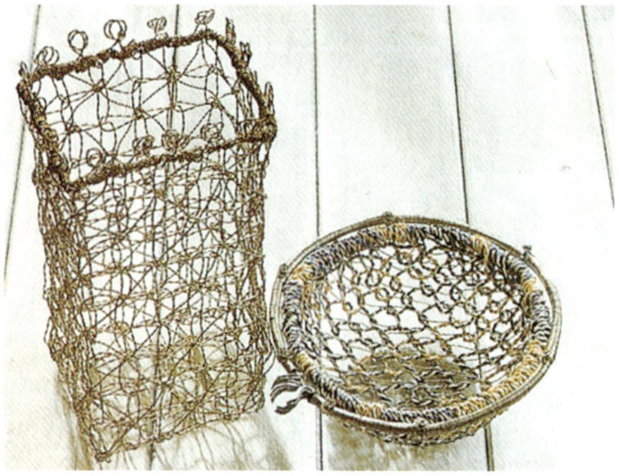

Above: BOWL AND CANNISTER
These pieces are made from painted and stitched paper and explore the techniques used in the plaited palm-leaf basketry characteristic of the Caribbean and Pacific.
JO GILMOUR

Left: WIRE BASKETS
Worked over a mould, these intricate baskets made from a variety of metal wires use several linking techniques in their construction.
HILARY BURNS

Above: "PEBBLES"
These pebble-shaped baskets were woven using a range of willow weaves. They were then coated inside with pine resin.
GERALDINE JAMES

Below: SCENT BOTTLE
This piece stands approximately 1 m (3 ft) tall. Made from willow dyed with indigo and fibre reactive dyes, it has a carved wooden stopper.
JOHN GALLOWAY

Above: BROWN WILLOW BOWL
Varying lengths of fine brown and white willow rods were drilled, then threaded together in a carefully planned grid formation with telephone wire, which was knotted to hold the layers together and create the bowl shape.
DAIL BEHENNAH

Right: LIDDED BASKET WITH HANDLE
Inspired by African basketry, this lidded, dyed cane basket is worked in waling. The applied surface decoration is dyed chair cane, as is the handle, where it is worked into a tubular, 4-strand plait.
ALEX BARRY

BASKETRY MATERIALS

THE BULK OF THE MATERIALS USED IN THIS BOOK ARE THOSE TRADITIONALLY USED IN BASKETWORK: NAMELY, CANE AND WILLOW. THE COMBINATION OF THESE MATERIALS IN SOME PROJECTS, AND THE ADDITION OF LESS TRADITIONAL MATERIALS IN OTHERS, GIVE THE PIECES A CONTEMPORARY FEEL.

Birch plywood Available from a good timber merchant, plywood that is 6-8 mm (¼–⅝ in) thick is the ideal thickness for a tray base. The quality of the wood means that it is unlikely to warp.

Cane Also known as rattan, this grows in many places around the world, but the vast majority imported for basket-making comes from South-East Asia, in particular, Indonesia and Malaysia.

Whole cane goes through several processes to extract the pith, which is known as centre cane. This is then milled to produce long strands of varying thickness, ranging from very fine (No 000 which is 1 mm [1/32 in] in diameter), up to the larger sizes of handle cane (which are around 10 mm [½ in] in diameter). The mid-range sizes include No 5 and No 8. Centre cane for basket-making is sold in ½ kilo (1 lb) hanks.

Whole cane has two layers of bark; part of the processing involves removing the shiny inner bark which is split into long strands of varying thickness: from No 0 (1.3 mm [1/30 in] wide) up to No 6 (3.7 mm [⅛ in]). Known as chair cane, it is used for caning chairs; anything above this thickness is known as glossy lapping cane.

Processed cane has a neutral, creamy colour but can be dyed easily.

Corrugated paper and cardboard This comes in many colours and thicknesses and is used for the greetings card project.

Willow Willow is sold in bolts, a bolt being a large bundle of rods with a circumference of 94 cm (37 in) when measured 5 cm (2 in) from the bottom. Bolts of willow are traditionally measured in feet, but for ease of use worldwide, both metric and imperial measurements have been provided. While all bolts of willow have the same circumference, the length and thickness of the rods vary, from 90 cm (3 ft) for the thinnest, through 1.2 m (4 ft), 1.5 m (5 ft), up to 1.8 m (6 ft) for the thickest. Larger sizes do exist but they are not used in this book. Different sizes of willow are used in different parts of a basket.

Willow is available in three different types: brown, buff and white.

Brown willow is the name given to willow that receives no additional processing after being cut and dried. The natural colours of the intact bark are beautiful and include green (Black Maul) and a reddish brown (Flanders Red). Brown willow is the cheapest to buy.

Buff willow has been boiled in large tanks for several hours after being cut. Tannin released from the bark during boiling dyes the rod the characteristic terracotta colour, which is revealed after the wet bark has been stripped off. Buff willow has a medium price range.

White willow is the most labour-intensive to produce. For white willow, the sap is allowed to rise and rods to shoot. The rising sap results in the bark loosening, when it is removed either by manually dragging the rods between two metal prongs called a "brake" or by using a mechanical brake. The stripped rods are a wonderful shade of white which mellows with age to a warm honey colour. White willow is the most expensive.

Wire Strong wire, of the thickness of coat-hanger wire, is used to make and attach the handle for the bicycle basket.

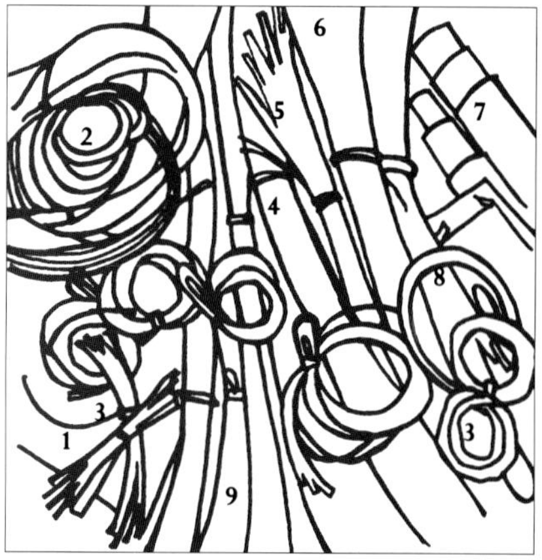

KEY
1 Birch plywood
2 Natural cane
3 Dyed cane
4 White willow
5 Buff willow
6 Brown willow
7 Corrugated paper
8 Thick wire
9 Dyed willow

EQUIPMENT AND OTHER MATERIALS

BASKETRY REQUIRES VERY LITTLE SPECIALIST EQUIPMENT. WITH THE EXCEPTION OF A VERY FEW, YOU WILL FIND YOU ALREADY OWN MOST OF THE ITEMS, OR YOU CAN IMPROVISE. SOME OF THE TOOLS – THE BODKINS AND KNIVES FOR EXAMPLE – NEED TO BE HANDLED WITH CAUTION.

Acrylic paint This "plastic"-based paint produces strong, vibrant colours, and is ideal for painting the base of the tray project. Powder or poster paint can also be used, followed by coats of varnish.
Beads These can be threaded onto cane and incorporated into the finished design.
Bodkin A bodkin is essential for piercing sticks when forming a slath. It is also used for creating channels in the weaving, when staking-up for example, and for opening up spaces between stakes.
Bradawl A bradawl can be used to pierce holes through materials which might damage the point of a bodkin. Take care when using this tool to direct it away from the hands and body.
Craft knife A professional basket-maker uses several traditional knives. However, a sharp craft knife, or a good quality penknife, is a good substitute.
Drill An electric or a hand drill with a 3–4 mm (⅛ in) drill bit are both suitable: the holes need to be large enough for No 10 cane to thread through.
Fishing line This is used to suspend the fish on the mobile project. Fishing line is sold in specialist angling shops. 0.125 mm line was used for the fish mobile, but any similar size would do the job just as well.
Grease pot Many professional willow basket-makers dip the end of their bodkin or stakes into a grease pot to make staking up easier – the grease helps the stake to slide into the base weaving. To make a grease pot, fill a pot with willow shavings and tallow.
Handle liners These are lengths of handle cane or thick willow rods cut into lengths with a slype (sloping cut) on one end. They are inserted into the basket to make a channel for the handle bow.
Hoop Make by forming a long willow rod into a ring by tying the first stage of a basic knot with the rod. Adjust the size of the hoop to the desired circumference of the basket at the border, and then wind the excess willow around the hoop.
Masking tape Use for temporarily holding stakes in place.
Metal file A small medium-grade file is sufficient for filing away rough edges.
Metal ruler and tape measure For measuring and ruling out straight lines.
Varnish Use to enhance the colour of the cane projects or to provide a protective coating. Use an acrylic or polyurethane varnish with a satin finish. Varnish must be brushed in well, otherwise it will drip. Always work in a well-ventilated room.
Rapping iron Used mainly for willow basketry, this is a heavy, metal tool used, among other things, for knocking down rows of weaving to keep the level even.
Round-nosed pliers These are needed for pinching stakes when bending cane to work a border. They are not that easy to find in a regular hardware store, but are available from some basketry suppliers.
Sandpaper Medium- or fine-grade sandpaper is needed for smoothing off rough splinters after drilling holes and for rounding off edges on plywood.
Scissors A good sharp pair of scissors, for cutting card (cardboard), wire, fishing line and so on, is essential.
Side cutters These are used for cutting cane. They should be as sharp as possible in order to obtain accurate, clean cuts.
String Several types of string are called for. Strong string is used for tying up the stakes when upsetting a cane basket and when tying baskets into oval shapes. Thinner string is used for marking the step-up, and it is helpful if this is a bright colour.
Weight Using a weight to hold down work in progress makes controlling the shape much easier.

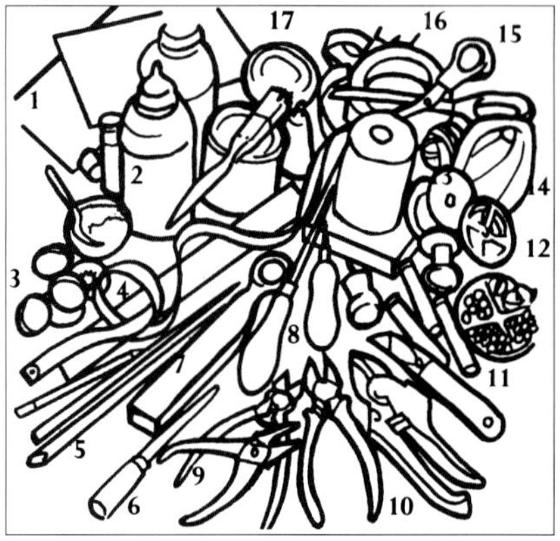

KEY
1 Sandpaper
2 Acrylic paint
3 Hot-water dyes
4 Tape measure and ruler
5 Handle liners
6 Metal file
7 Rapping iron
8 Bodkins
9 Pliers (round-nosed and straight)
10 Side cutters
11 Craft knife
12 Beads
13 Fishing line
14 String
15 Scissors
16 Masking tape
17 Varnish

STANLEY

BASIC TECHNIQUES

IN SPITE OF THE LIMITED PERCEPTION MANY PEOPLE HAVE OF IT, BASKETRY IS A HIGHLY DEVELOPED AND SKILLED CRAFT. FAMILIARITY WITH THE TECHNIQUES DESCRIBED ON THE FOLLOWING PAGES IS ESSENTIAL IN ORDER TO MAKE THE PROJECTS IN THIS BOOK SUCCESSFULLY, AND IT WILL BE NECESSARY TO REFER BACK TO THEM FREQUENTLY. BEGIN WITH THE SIMPLER PROJECTS AND GRADUALLY BUILD UP YOUR SKILLS IN ORDER TO ACHIEVE SATISFYING RESULTS.

PREPARING CANE FOR WORKING

Cane needs to be soaked because in its dry state it is prone to crack. Soaking times depend on the thickness of the cane and the temperature of the water. The thicker sizes of cane will need a maximum of 5–10 minutes soaking in hottish water – the thinner the cane and the hotter the water the less is needed. As a rough guide, if the cane can bend in a right angle without cracking, it is ready. Keep cane damp with a plant spray while working, and leave pieces in an airy place to dry. Cut cane at an angle, as it is often useful to have a pointed end, for example when staking up a base.

DYING CANE

When dying cane work in a well-ventilated room, wearing a mask and rubber gloves and apron to protect your clothes. Never use a container that will be used for food, as toxic traces can remain. Always read and follow the dye manufacturer's instructions and safety advice.

Method

Take 2–3 strands of cane from a hank and wrap them into a loose bundle (to avoid a tie-dye effect). Soak the bundles in water for a few minutes.

Prepare the dye solution, following the manufacturer's instructions.

Add a few bundles of cane at a time to the dye and keep stirring with a stick to ensure that the cane dyes evenly. When the cane has reached the colour you desire, rinse it thoroughly under running water.

RANDING

Randing is a weave worked with 1 weaver; however, this 1 weaver can be made up of 1, 2, 3 or even 4 strands. Except in the first instance, the weavers are always worked as 1 in a "ribbon" formation.

Lay in 1 weaver behind a stake (a stake and bye-stake are treated as 1 unless otherwise stated) and weave it in front of 1 stake, behind 1 stake and so on.

Join when the end of a weaver begins to run out. Leave the short end behind a stake. Lay in the end of the new weaver behind the same stake and continue weaving. Later, trim off the ends of the weavers, making sure that the trimmed ends are lying over the stake.

PACKING

Packing is a randing weave that is usually worked with one weaver. It is often used to build up an area of a basket to alter the shape and/or create colour patterns. Packing can be worked over both an even and an odd number of stakes.

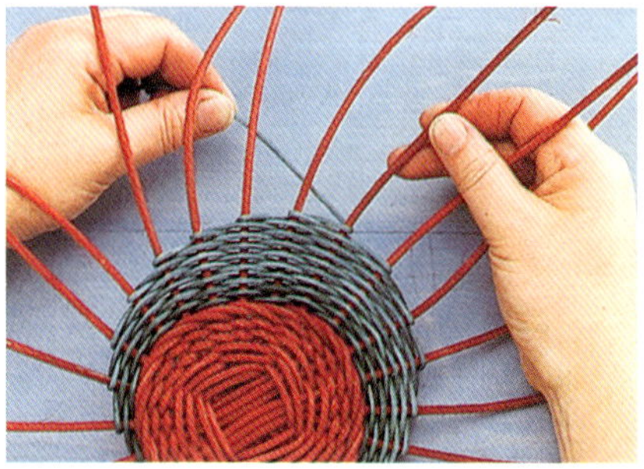

1 Lay in a weaver between 2 stakes. The stake the end of the weaver lies behind will be stake 1. Rand over a chosen number of stakes (18 are shown in the photograph). On reaching the last stake, weave around this stake ready to weave back in the opposite direction.

Rand backwards and forwards across the stakes, but turn around 1 stake less at the end of each row until only 2 stakes remain. After working around the last 2 stakes, leave the end of the weaver at the back of the work.

PAIRING

Pairing is a weave which uses 2 weavers and is used on all parts of a basket. When worked with dyed weavers it can produce a range of colour patterns.

1 Lay in 2 weavers in 2 consecutive spaces. Take the left-hand weaver in front of the stake immediately to its right, over the right-hand weaver, behind the 2nd stake to the right, and out to the front again; the left-hand weaver has now become the right-hand weaver. Now take the left-hand weaver in front of 1, behind 1, and so on.

2 There is more than one way to join in pairing, but this book only uses a cross-over join. When a weaver needs joining ensure that it is the left-hand of the pair. Lift up the weaving a little, insert a new weaver in the same space as the existing weaver, placing it under and slightly to the left of the weaver being joined. Push down the weaving again. Pick up the new weaver, and, working over the end of the weaver being replaced, continue pairing.

3 To complete, work the last stroke but, as the left-hand weaver is brought to the front, thread it under the top strand of the row below, to secure it. The second strand is trapped, and so secured, by the one you have just threaded.

WALING

Waling is another weave that can be used on all parts of a basket. It is worked with 3, or more, weavers at a time. It is a strong weave and is often used to change and/or control the shape of a basket.

Variations in colour and textural patterns can be achieved by varying the number of stakes the weave is worked over, the number of colours used, or the number of strands used as one weaver, that is in a "ribbon formation".

3-rod waling

1 Lay in 3 weavers into 3 consecutive spaces. Tie a marker on to the stake immediately to the left of the left-hand weaver. Take the left-hand weaver (turquoise in the photograph) and work it in front of 2 stakes and behind 1 stake. The turquoise weaver will now be the right-hand weaver.

2 Take the weaver which is now on the left (purple) and work it in front of 2, behind 1. Next take the pink weaver, which is now on the left, and work it in front of 2, behind 1. Continue, always working with the left-hand weaver, in front of 2 stakes, behind 1 stake.

Working a 3-rod step-up

When working waling weaves in cane, it is advisable to work a step-up at the end of each row. This completes each row, prevents the weave spiralling, and so produces a level height.

1 At the end of a row, that is, when the right-hand weaver is in the space immediately to the left of the marked stake, begin to work the step-up. This is done by taking the right-hand weaver (pink) and working it in front of 2 behind 1.

2 Next, take the middle weaver (purple), and finally the left-hand weaver (turquoise), working them both in front of 2 behind 1. At this point, the step-up will be complete. The weavers will be in position to begin the next row with the left-hand weaver (turquoise) in the space immediately to the right of the marked stake, ready to work in front of 2, behind 1, and so on.

Joining in 3-rod waling

1 Always join when the short end is on the left. Pull back the short end a little towards the left. Insert the new weaver under the other 2 weavers, and into the space between the short end and the stake to its right. The new weaver will then work as usual, in front of 2, behind 1.

Completing 3-rod waling

1 At the end of a block of waling work a step-up. Then thread each weaver under the top 2 strands of the row below, keeping them in the spaces that they would normally come out of.

4-rod waling variations

4-rod waling is worked in the same way as 3-rod waling, but with 4 weavers. The weavers may be worked in front of 3 (instead of 2) behind 1, or in front of 2 behind 2. The principle of the step-up is the same, only with 4 stages. When completing 4-rod waling, work a 4-rod step-up and thread each weaver under the top 3 strands of the row below.

WEAVING A ROUND BASE

The number of sticks used to make a slath, the name given to the cross of sticks when they have been pierced and threaded, varies according to the size and shape of the basket being made. The number of sticks used in the example shown here is for an average-sized basket.

Making a 4-through-4 slath

1 Cut 8 sticks, and soak them in warm water for 5–10 minutes to soften them. Pierce 4 of them through the centre, by threading them on to a bodkin.

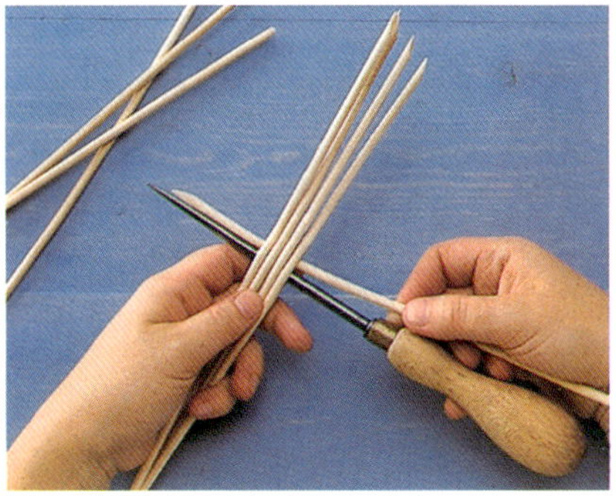

2 Thread the 5th stick through the 4 pierced sticks; remove the bodkin. Thread the remaining 3 sticks through the pierced sticks. You will now have a 4-through-4 slath.

Tying in the slath

1 Take a soaked length of cane and loop it around one "arm" of the slath. This first stage of "tying in the slath" will look best if the 1st loop lies parallel to the pierced sticks. You will have 2 weavers, 1 on either side of the "arm" – 1 on the left and 1 on the right. Hold down the right-hand strand of the weaver across the slath with the thumb of your left hand. Take the left-hand strand of the weaver in your right hand, and work it across the 1st "arm" of the slath, then down behind the 2nd "arm". Rotate the slath a quarter turn anti-clockwise (counterclockwise).

2 Again, while holding down the right-hand weaver, work the left-hand weaver in front of the top "arm" and then down behind the next "arm". Keep the weaving as tight and even as possible. Work 2 rows like this, after which the process will be complete. The weave used for tying in the slath and for weaving the remainder of the base is called pairing.

Weaving the base

1 Begin opening out the sticks (arms of the slath) into pairs, using the same pairing weave as for tying in the slath. Pull the sticks apart firmly so that the weaving can go down into the spaces between the sticks, enabling them to be opened out evenly and the weaving to remain tight.

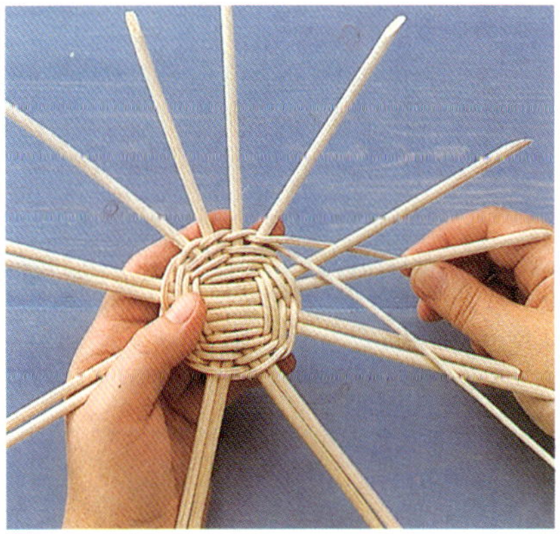

2 After 2 rows, begin opening out the sticks into singles. As the left-hand weaver is worked, pull it firmly downwards at the back before bringing it back up to the front to keep the weaving tight.

While weaving the base, push the sticks away from you slightly in order to create a slightly domed shape: the base should have the same curve as an upturned saucer. Keep the sticks as evenly spaced as possible.

Completing pairing on a base

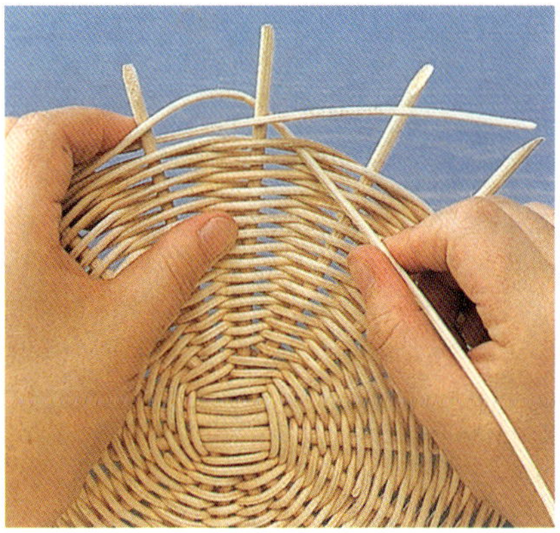

1 Complete pairing above where you began – tying in the slath or working the siding – by threading the left-hand weaver under the top strand of the row below. The second strand is automatically trapped, and so secured, by the one you have just threaded.

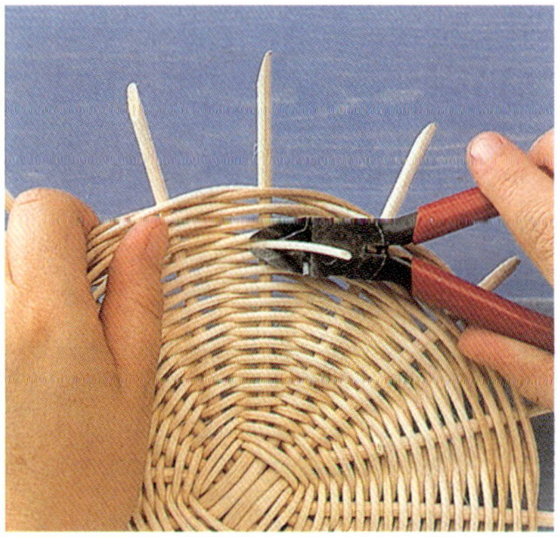

2 Trim off the ends of the weavers as follows: the left-hand weaver, which was threaded away, is cut off so that it lies over the weavers; the other is cut off so that it lies over a stake, so preventing the weavers from unravelling. Trim off the ends of any joins on both sides of the base so that the cut ends lie over a stake. Generally, it is better to trim off on the base after the base has been staked up.

UPSETTING THE BASKET

Staking Up

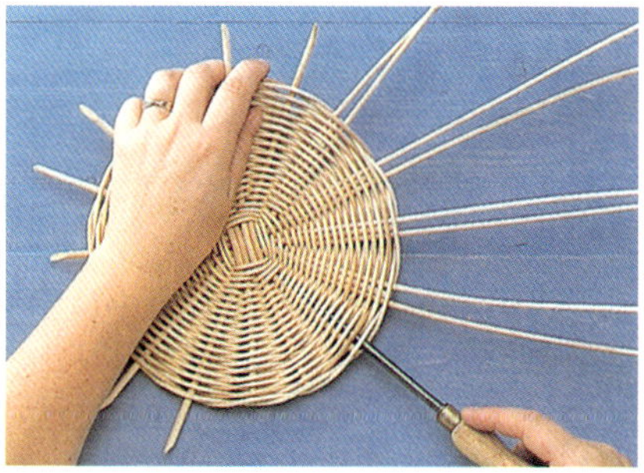

1 Using side cutters, cut off 3 or 4 sticks as close to the weaving as possible; if you trim more at a time, the weaving may unravel. Dip the base and the stakes in water until they are no longer brittle, but don't soak either for any length of time or staking up will become difficult. Insert the stakes, one on either side of each stick. Push them down as far as possible, ideally to where the sticks are opened out to singles. If necessary use the bodkin to open up a channel in the weaving.

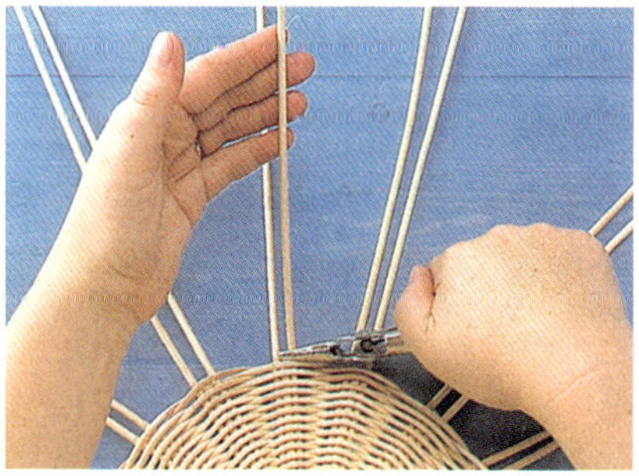

2 When all the stakes are inserted, soak them for 5–10 minutes. Using round-nosed pliers, pinch the stakes as close to the base weaving as possible; make sure the pliers are in the same position as shown in the photograph. Then bend the stakes upwards and tie them tightly together in a bunch with string, about 30 cm (12 in) above the slath.

Working an upsett

The instructions given here are for working a 4-rod upsett. If you were working a 3-rod upsett, you would insert 3 weavers to the left of 3 consecutive stakes. Then you would work a 3-rod wale (with the weavers travelling in front of 2 stakes, behind 1), and a 3-rod step-up, and then complete as for 3-rod waling.

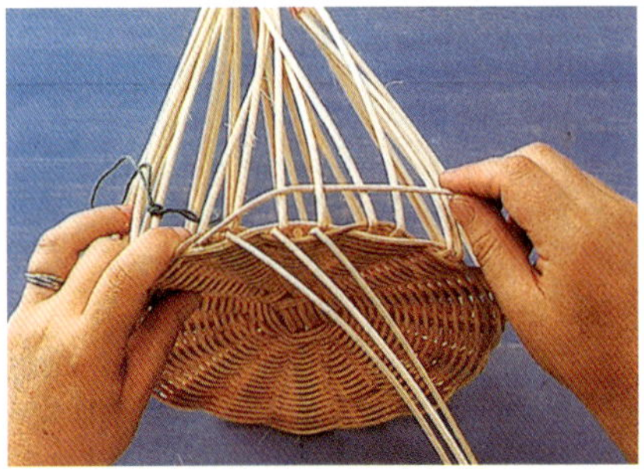

1 Turn the base on its side and insert 4 weavers to the left of 4 *consecutive stakes*. Mark the step-up on the stake to the left of the left-hand weaver. Keep the base on its side, and begin working a 4-rod wale. Keep this 1st row of waling as close to the base weaving as possible. As you weave, pull apart the stakes, using the weaving to spread them around the base.

2 At the end of the row work a step-up. The 4-rod step-up shown here is worked in the same way as a 3-rod step-up, except that it has 4 stages. Each weaver travels in front of 3, behind 1, but in reverse order, that is from right to left. With the basket on its base, add a weight to anchor the basket while working.

Begin working the 2nd row of waling, bearing in mind that it is the 1st rows of weaving that determine the shape of a basket. For example, to achieve a cylindrical basket, the stakes need to be held at a 92-degree angle to the base (if the stakes were at a 90-degree angle to the base, an optical illusion would occur, with the basket appearing narrower at the top than the bottom.)

3 Work about 4 or 5 rows of waling, then complete the waling by working a step-up. Here a 4-rod step-up is worked. Thread each weaver under the top 3 strands of the row below.

4 Insert a bye-stake into the upsett waling to the right of every stake then work the siding of the basket with your chosen weave(s). Bye-stakes provide additional rigidity and strength to a cane basket. Normally they are the same length as the height of the basket, and with some exceptions they are always placed on the right of the stakes.

5 When the side weaving is complete, cut off the bye-stakes as close as possible to the weaving, using side cutters. Push down on the weaving a little with the cutters to ensure as close a cut as possible.

6 Soak the stakes again for 5–10 minutes, then pinch them with round-nosed pliers immediately above the weaving.

WORKING A 3-ROD BORDER

1 Starting at any point, bend down one of the upright stakes (a) behind the upright stake immediately to its right (b); then bring this upright (b) down behind the next upright to the right (c) and so on until 3 upright stakes have been brought down behind the upright to their right.

2 Pick up the left-hand stake (a) of the 3 brought-down stakes. Take it in front of the 1st upright stake to its right (d), then behind the 2nd upright stake to its right (e). Make an exaggerated curve in the cane (a), as illustrated, as this will be important when completing the border. Next, bring the 1st, left-hand upright (d) down to lie next to and behind the left-hand brought-down stake (a), which has just been worked, to form a pair – (a) and (d).

3 Work stake (b) in front of the next upright (e) and behind the upright after that (f). Bring upright (e) down behind upright (f) to form a pair with (b). Then work stake (c) in front of (f) and behind (g); bring (f) down behind (g) to form a pair with (c). Now 3 pairs of stakes have been brought down.

4 Take the right-hand stake (d) of the left-hand pair of stakes, and work it in front of upright (g), behind upright (h).

5 Bring upright (g) down to make a pair with (d). You should now have a single stake at the left, with 3 pairs to its right. Continue working the border until only 1 upright remains. Always take the right-hand stake of the left-hand pair, and work it in front of 1 upright, behind 1 upright, and then bring the left-hand upright down to make a pair.

6 Take the right-hand stake of the left-hand pair and work it in front of the remaining upright. Then take it "behind" what would have been the next upright (this was the 1st upright to be brought down) by threading it under the "elbow" of the brought-down stake.

7 Bring down the remaining upright and thread it under the same elbow to form a pair.

8 The elbows of the 1st 3 stakes to be brought down are still "singles" – all the others are pairs. To complete the border, take the right-hand stake of the 3 remaining pairs to make these single elbows into pairs. The right-hand stake of the left-hand pair will form a pair with the left-hand single elbow, and so on.

So, thread the right-hand stake (x) of the left-hand pair to the inside of the basket alongside the elbow of stake (a) – it will thread between the weaving and the border. Then thread it to the outside again by taking it behind and under stake (b), that is between the weaving and the border. Gently pull the stake (x) to the front of the elbow of stake (a).

9 The final 2 stages are very similar to Step 8. Take stake (y) and thread it alongside the elbow of stake (b), then behind and under the elbow of stake (c), between the weaving and the border. Pull gently to the front.

10 Take stake (z) and thread it alongside the elbow of stake (c), then behind and under the elbow of stake (d), between the weaving and the border. Pull gently to the front. There should now be a single stake coming out of every space. These stakes can either be trimmed off or a follow-on border can be worked.

WORKING A FOLLOW-ON BORDER

Follow-on borders are worked for decoration; to avoid having the cut ends of stakes catch clothes, etc; or to strengthen.

To work a simple follow-on border, take a stake (a) under the 2 stakes to its right (b) and (c), and thread it to the inside between the weaving and the border through the same space that stake (c) comes out of. Trim off the stakes on the inside, using side cutters.

Working a 4-rod border

The method is almost identical to a 3-rod border, but here, 4 stakes are brought down in the 1st stage, 4 pairs are created in the 2nd stage and, in the final stage, there are 4 "singles" to be made into pairs.

WILLOW TECHNIQUES

Willow rods curve and taper. The outside curve is known as the back, and the inside the belly. The thick end of the rod is known as the butt and the thin end the tip. When working with willow, you will need to alternate tips and butts, to make the weaving even.

PREPARING WILLOW FOR WORKING

Willow must be soaked in water for several hours or even days, depending on the size and type. It is then wrapped up in a cloth and mellowed to ensure that the innermost parts become fully pliable. Buff and white willow should be mellowed for a few hours depending on the size, and brown willow for at least 8–12 hours.

Soaking times

Size	*Buff and White*	*Brown*
90 cm (3 ft)	½–1 hour	2 days
1.2 m (4 ft)	1–1½ hours	3 days
1.5 m (5 ft)	1½–2 hours	4 days
1.8 m (6 ft)	2–3 hours	5 days

DYING WILLOW

Use fibre-reactive dyes, mixed according to the manufacturer's instructions. Mix to a paste with hot water. Make a dye bath: securely seal off one end of a 10 cm (4 in) diameter soil pipe, using 1.2 m (4 ft) length for 90 cm (3 ft) willow, and so on. Add more hot water to the paste, then pour in to the pipe. Put in the dry willow, then top up with water. (Do not pack too tightly or the dye will not be even). Allow 1 hour drying time for the 1st batch, 2 hours for the 2nd etc, until the dye is exhausted. Remove the willow and leave to dry for about 12 hours, soak and rinse for ½ an hour then allow to dry again. Soak and mellow as usual before use.

Making the slath
When making the slath with willow, pierce and thread the sticks as for cane. Thread a stick through the splits at right angles to the 1st group of sticks. Thread through the remaining sticks, making sure butts and tips (thick and thin ends) alternate.

Tying in the slath
Choose 2 fine long rods and push the tips down through the split sticks to the left-hand side of the unsplit sticks. Hold the slath with these 2 rods to the top left of the unsplit sticks and the split ones horizontal. Take 1 round the back of the unsplit sticks and bring back to the front (*) Take the left of the 2 rods in front of the 3 sticks, to the back above the 2nd rod and behind the 3 sticks projecting to the right and back to the front. Turn the slath a ¼ turn anti-clockwise. Repeat from (*) until you have 2 ties round each section of the slath.

Opening out with pairing
Opening out the stakes is very similar to cane. Continue pairing round the base to the diameter required, pushing the stakes away in order to create a shallow dome.

Joining
When joining in willow, all rods are joined at the same time, butts to butts and tips to tips. With 3-rod waling, when the 1st 3 rods are running out, join new butts to the old ones: pull the left-hand butt to the left and push a new butt beside and to the right of it. Leaving 2-3 cm (1 ½ in) of the new rod on the inside, work the new rod in front of 2, behind 1. Join the other 2 rods in the same way (all 3 are joined simultaneously) and continue weaving to tips. Tip to tip joins are made in the same way. Pairing joins are made as for waling, except that only 2 rods will be joined.

Finishing the base
Weaving must end with tips to ensure a round base. To finish, thread one tip up through the weaving of the row below. This will prevent the weavers unravelling.

Cutting a slype
A slype is a 2.5 cm (1 in) long diagonal cut or pair of cuts made at the butt end of a willow rod. It slims the rod so it can be pushed into a basket base, or beside a broken stake. Hold the rod firmly with the left hand, about 10 cm (4 in) behind the butt. Tuck the rest of the rod under your left arm. Use a sharp knife to make a diagonal cut.

Staking up
Select rods of the same thickness, slyping them at the butt end. Push in the rods with the slyped surface to the top of the base (ie away from you)

Pricking up
Turn the base over, dome upwards. Push a knife point a little way into a stake, close to the base and turn it about 90 degrees while lifting the rod up. This will break up the fibre of the rod, allowing it to bend without cracking.

Working a 3-rod upsett
This is worked similarly to cane. Start a 3-rod wale by inserting the tips into the base weaving to the left of 3 consecutive stakes. With the base on its side, bend the 3 rods down. The weavers are worked as for cane. Becasue willow rods taper, no step-up is worked.

Siding
Various weaves can be used, among them French randing, English randing and slewing. A band of waling to make the upsett waling is usually put on before the border is worked.

Chasing
To produce even weaving in waling, it is sometimes necessary to work with 2 sets of weavers simultaneously: lay the tips of 3 or 4 rods into 3 or 4 consecutive spaces and wale half way round the basket. Insert 3 or 4 more tips into 3 consecutive spaces to the right of where the 1st 3 weavers now are. Continue waling with the 2nd set of weavers until you catch up with the 1st set. Drop the 2nd set of weavers and resume weaving with the 1st set, until you catch up again with the 2nd and so on. One set of weavers *never* overtakes the other.

Borders.
Variations of rod borders are explained in the individual willow projects.

GREETINGS CARD

TO MINIMIZE WASTAGE, PROFESSIONAL BASKET-MAKERS HAVE ALWAYS MADE THE BEST POSSIBLE USE OF THEIR MATERIALS – BASKET-MAKING HAS NEVER BEEN A WELL-PAID PROFESSION. SOME WEAVES EVEN EVOLVED THROUGH A NEED TO MAKE WILLOW STRETCH AS FAR AS POSSIBLE. THE DESIGN OF THIS CARD KEEPS THIS PHILOSOPHY IN MIND BY USING UP OFF-CUTS (SCRAPS) OF WILLOW; CANE OFF-CUTS COULD JUST AS EASILY BE USED. SMALLER VERSIONS OF THE CARD CAN BE MADE AS GIFT-TAGS, USING THINNER CANE OR WILLOW, WHILE LARGE VERSIONS COULD MAKE USE OF THICKER OFF-CUTS.

1 Draw and cut out a 24 x 16.5 cm (9½ x 6½ in) rectangle on a sheet of corrugated cardboard and another on the thin card (cardboard). Fold each in half. Glue the two sheets together and leave to dry. Cut an 11.5 x 8 cm (4½ x 3¼ in) rectangle from the remaining sheet of corrugated cardboard.

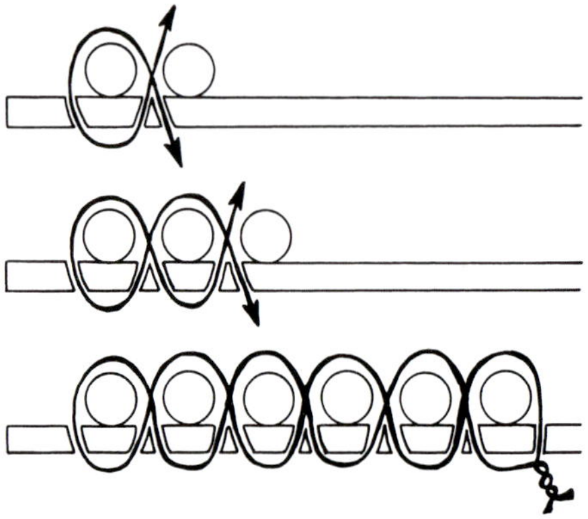

2 Arrange the willow off-cuts (scraps) on masking tape. Put a stripe of glue down the centre of the small rectangle, the length of the line of willow off-cuts. Position the 1st piece of willow and hold it down in the centre. Referring to the diagram, begin working the 1st line of cobbler's stitch with copper wire to hold the off-cut in place.

3 Secure the other end of the willow off-cuts with a 2nd line of stitching.

4 Tie off the ends of copper wire on the back of the card.

5 Glue the decorated sheet of card to the front of the folded greetings card.

MATERIALS AND EQUIPMENT YOU WILL NEED

PENCIL • RULER • THIN SINGLE-FACED CORRUGATED CARDBOARD, IN 2 COLOURS • THIN CARD (CARDBOARD) • SCISSORS • GLUE STICK • WILLOW OFF-CUTS (SCRAPS), DYED IN SEVERAL COLOURS • MASKING TAPE • NEEDLE • FINE COPPER WIRE

BROWN WILLOW FAN

THESE FANS ARE AN EXCELLENT PROJECT TO MAKE WITH CHILDREN. THEY ARE QUICK AND EASY TO MAKE AND BECAUSE BROWN WILLOW IS FAIRLY ROBUST, IT CAN WITHSTAND BEING HANDLED BY INEXPERIENCED LITTLE HANDS, OR INDEED ANYONE WISHING TO FAMILIARIZE THEMSELVES WITH THE FEEL OF BROWN WILLOW.

1 Take 14 150 cm (5 ft) rods, including 1 thinner than the others. Bind them about 15 cm (6 in) from the butt ends, with the thinner rod near the back on the left. To bind, take a thin 90 cm (3 ft) rod and hold it together with the bundle, with the butt end pointing upwards and the long end down. Wrap the long end clockwise around the bundle a few times, enclosing the wrapping rod in the binding. With a bodkin, make a channel alongside the enclosed section of the wrapping rod, then thread the tip of this rod down beside the butt end. Pull the ends to tighten the binding and trim the ends. Holding the thin rod at the back, separate the other rods into 3 groups of 4, 5 and 4 rods. Bring the thin rod round the left-hand group to the front, weave over the left and behind the central group, over and round the right-hand group.

2 Continue randing around these 3 groups, joining in new 90 cm (3 ft) rods at the back as necessary. Do not weave around the 2 outer groups too tightly or they will not be able to fan out.

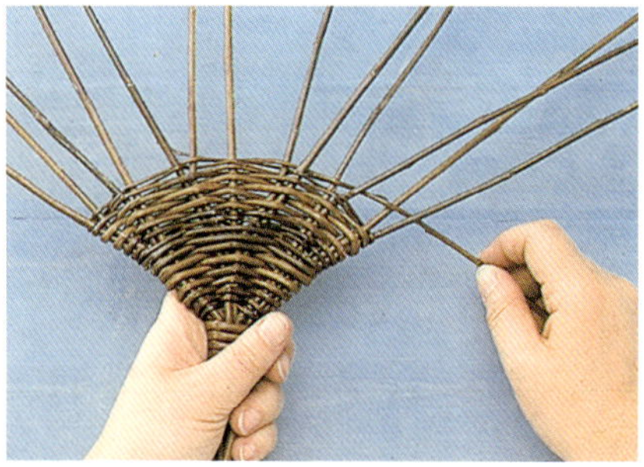

3 After 6 or 7 rows, open out the rods into 3 pairs on either side of a central single rod and continue randing around the pairs. Avoid joining in new rods near the outer pairs. After another 9 or 10 rows, open the pairs to singles.

4 Rand for 30–35 rows, until the fan is about 11.5–13 cm (4½–5 in) high, with the stakes no more than 4.5 cm (1¾ in) apart. With the front facing you, and working from left to right, weave the left-hand stake in front and behind the remaining upright stakes to lie behind the stake on the right.

5 Weave the other stakes in the same way, working from left to right. Bend down the last stake on the right to lie with the others in the group. Pick up the 1st border stake worked, at the bottom of the group, bring it up from behind the right-hand stake, then wrap up around the front of the group, down behind and so on, as tightly as possible, for about 5 wraps.

6 Turn the work over and thread the end of the stake back through the binding in much the same way that the binding was worked in Step 1. Cut off the ends of the bundle of stakes about 2.5 cm (1 in) from the binding. Trim off all joins at the back so that they lie over a stake.

MATERIALS AND EQUIPMENT YOU WILL NEED

150 CM (5 FT) BROWN WILLOW RODS • 90 CM (3 FT) BROWN WILLOW RODS • BODKIN • SIDE CUTTERS • TAPE MEASURE

Table Mat

The techniques used for making this project are very much the same as for weaving a base, so why not make a set of mats for your kitchen or dining table while perfecting your base and 3-rod border skills? The mats could be identical or you could experiment with patterns that can be achieved with pairing when the position of the dyed weavers is changed. Choose a range of colours that will match or complement the room and/or tableware. Even if the patterns differ from mat to mat, the colour scheme will pull the set together.

1 Cut 8 x 28 cm (11 in) sticks from the No 10 cane and make a 4-through-4 slath. Using a strand of the green No 5 cane, tie in the slath with 2 rows of pairing. On the 3rd row open out the sticks into pairs and on the 4th row open them out into singles. At the beginning of the 5th row join in a turquoise weaver to replace one of the green weavers.

2 Continue weaving with both colours for 4 or 5 rows. Cut 32 x 38 cm (15 in) border stakes from the turquoise No 10 cane and insert them to the left-hand side of each stick, pushing them down to where the 2-colour weaving begins. Continue weaving, keeping the work flat and ensuring the stakes remain evenly spaced.

3 Work 12 more rows of the 2-colour weaving, then swap the position of both weavers and work another 6 rows. Complete the pairing.

4 Trim off the sticks, then soak the border stakes. With the wrong side of the mat facing you, pinch down each stake to the right. Keeping the wrong side facing, work a 3-rod border. Make sure that no gap occurs between the weaving and the border on the right side of the mat.

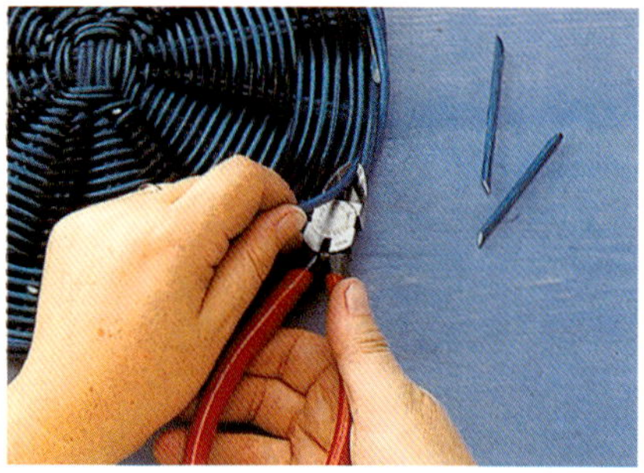

5 Trim off the end of each border stake where it lies over another stake. Finally, varnish the mat and leave to dry.

Materials and Equipment You Will Need

Side Cutters • Tape measure • No 10 cane, dyed turquoise, for the sticks and border stakes • Bodkin • No 5 cane, dyed green and turquoise, for the weavers • Round-nosed pliers • Varnish and brush

Stars

These star decorations make use of willow off-cuts (scraps), which ideally should be slightly thinner than a pencil or ballpoint pen. If you were planning to make a lot of stars, however, it would be worth dyeing up batches of willow, especially if you wanted to decorate a whole tree with the same colour. For a really Christmassy feel, the stars could be painted with a little glue and sprinkled with glitter.

1 Cut 5 x 23 cm (9 in) sticks from the willow. Tie 2 sticks tightly together about 4 cm (1½ in) from the ends, using copper wire. The left-hand stick should lie on top of and across the right-hand stick. Refer to the diagram for the correct over and under sequence of tying sticks.

2 Add the 3rd and 4th sticks, positioning and tying as shown. If necessary, use masking tape to hold the sticks in place while they are being tied.

3 Tie on the 5th stick. Gently adjust the shape of the star – it will not be a perfect shape – and tighten the ties if necessary.

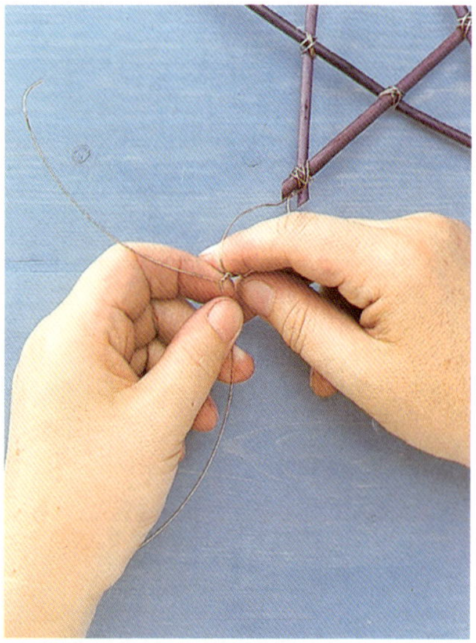

4 Decide which point of the star will look best at the top then tie a loop of copper wire about 15 cm (6 in) long at this point, for hanging the star.

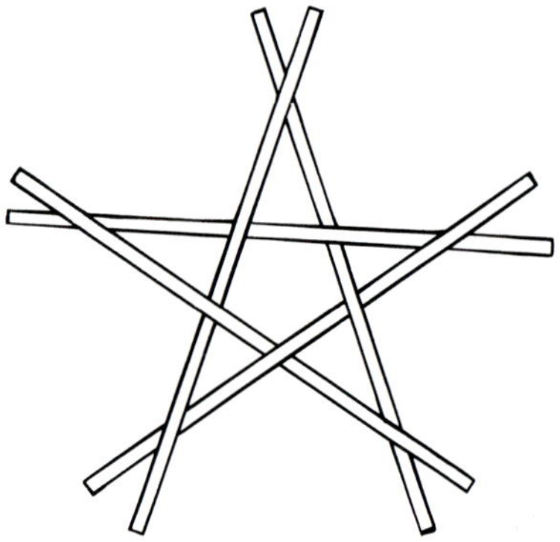

Materials and Equipment You Will Need

Side cutters • Tape measure • 1.2.–1.5 m (4–5 ft) willow rods, dyed • Copper wire • Scissors • Masking tape (optional)

HEDGEROW RING

CUT FROM THE HEDGEROW, THIS RUSTIC WREATH BRINGS THE FRESHNESS OF OUTDOORS INTO THE HOME. IT IS BASED ON LONG STRANDS OF PLIABLE BRANCHES, WHICH COULD BE WILLOW OR OTHER SUITABLE HEDGEROW RODS, BUILT UP INTO A CRISS-CROSSING FRAMEWORK. THE BRANCHES NEED TO BE HARVESTED A FEW WEEKS BEFORE USE TO ALLOW SOME OF THE SAP TO EVAPORATE BEFORE THEY ARE SHAPED.

1 Twist the butt end of a 1.8 m (6 ft) rod gently into a 30 cm (12 in) diameter hoop and tie it into a loose knot. Wind the tip end round in a gentle curve. Wrap a 2nd 1.8 m (6 ft) rod round the 1st hoop to strengthen it. Start with the butt end on the opposite side and wrap it in the opposite direction, pulling the tip end gently through the hoop. Trim all the ends at an angle. Make another hoop as above and tie the 2 together with string at several points.

2 Make 2 smaller hoops in the same way, 25 cm (10 in) in diameter. Fit these inside the 1st hoop and tie them all together at several points with string.

3 Take a piece of the vine and, starting with the thickest end, wrap it around the core. Try to make as many turns as possible while retaining a natural look.

4 Wrap a 2nd piece of vine in the opposite direction. Continue to build up the shape, winding first one way and then the other, until you are happy with the bulk of the ring.

5 Carefully thread ivy through the gaps in the vine in a random way, without damaging the leaves. Tie on pieces of string as decoration and shred the ends.

MATERIALS AND EQUIPMENT YOU WILL NEED

8 x 1.8 M (6 FT) LENGTHS OF PLIABLE MATERIAL: WILLOW OR OTHER HEDGEROW RODS • TAPE MEASURE • SECATEURS (SHEARS) • NATURAL STRING: JUTE, SEAGRASS OR OTHER • VINE OR CLIMBER MATERIAL • TRAILING IVY WITH SMALL LEAVES

Lollipop Heart

Stand this heart among your potted plants, or make larger ones to decorate your flower beds for the summer. Bring them inside during winter to protect them. The centre of this delightful heart motif can be filled with a random weave of any found material, as long as you keep it light and airy. Garden or hedgerow vines or climbers with tendrils, such as Virginia creeper or hops, work well.

1 Twist the butt end of a 1.5 m (5 ft) willow rod gently into an 18 cm (7 in) diameter hoop and tie it into a loose knot. Wrap the tip end gently round the hoop. Wrap the 2nd rod round the hoop. Start with the butt end on the opposite side and wrap it in the opposite direction, pulling the tip end through the hoop. Trim all the ends at an angle.

2 Tie the butt ends of the 1.2 m (4 ft) rods with string. Tension this end and make a 3-strand plait (braid) 15 cm (6 in) long, using doubled willows. Keep the plait flat by curving the rods round the bends in one plane.

3 Divide the rods of the plait into 2 sets of 3, taking 1 rod from each of the doubled rods of the plait. Place the hoop between the 2 groups.

4 Twist the 2 groups over each other twice to make a rope. Enclose the opposite side of the hoop and divide the rods into 2 groups again.

5 Bring the ends of the groups around into a heart shape, twisting as you go. Catch in the sides of the hoop as you come round. Using a bodkin, thread the ends into the plait following the weave.

6 Push the end of the straight hedgerow stick into the top of the heart then remove the string tie and bind as described in the willow fan. Fill in the heart shape with a random weave in trailing materials.

Materials and Equipment You Will Need

2 x 1.5 m (5 ft) brown willow rods • Tape measure • Secateurs (shears) • String • 6 x 1.2 m (4 ft) brown willow rods • Bodkin • 46 cm (18 in) straight hedgerow stick with attractive bark, such as hazel or cherry • 90 cm (3 ft) slender brown willow rod • Trailing materials such as Virginia creeper or hops

FISH PLATTER

MAKE A FISH-SHAPED DISH USING WILLOW. HERE, THE DISH IS MADE MORE DECORATIVE WITH AN OPEN-WORK WEAVE, BUT IT COULD EASILY BE MADE INTO A MORE SUBSTANTIAL PLATTER BY USING A SOLID WEAVE. YOU COULD WEAVE IN STRIPS OF BARK OR PLAITED (BRAIDED) LEAVES TO CREATE A SCALY TEXTURE.

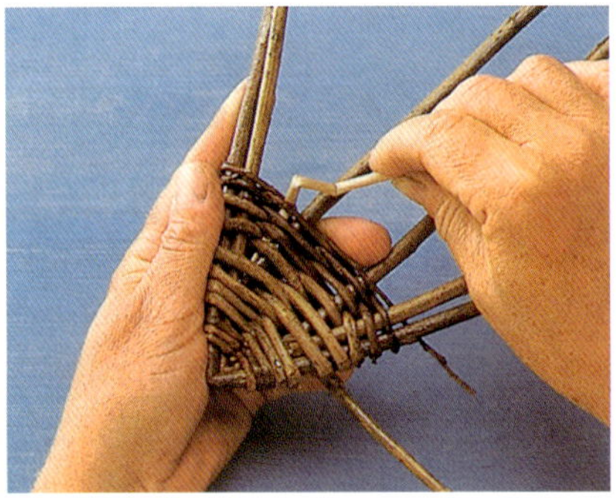

1 Follow Steps 1–3 of the Christmas Door Decoration, but work a concave platter shape, using the brown willow rods for the weaving. Work until the weaving measures 18 cm (7 in).

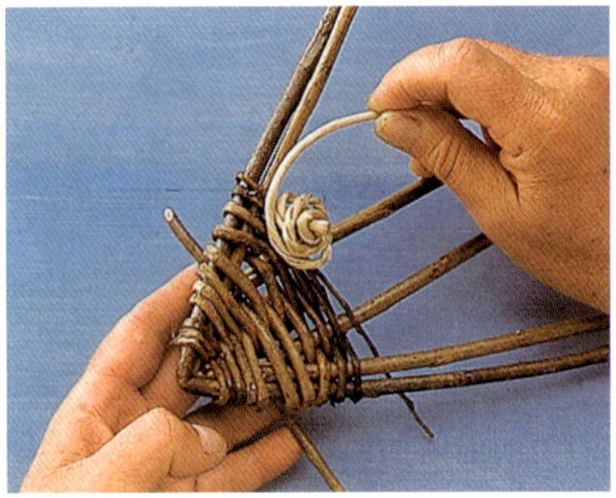

2 Insert a white rod into the weaving to start the eye. Kink the rod into an inverted V-shape and bind this round with the remainder of the rod, twisting it like a rope. Use a bodkin to thread away the end into the weaving.

3 Using a bodkin, widen the space at the top of the eye, push the tip of a new weaver though it, then weave it into the body of the platter to secure the wraps of the eye.

4 Continue to weave, using random colours and joining ends tip to tip and butt to butt, halfway along the body. To help shape the fish, tape the stakes together at the end of the body, leaving enough tips to make the tail. Trim off the thicker stakes.

5 Continue weaving until three-quarters of the body has been worked. With a long rod, work a figure-of-eight weave over the stakes. Push the butt end into the weaving and work up to the tape. Replace it with a wrap made from a fine willow rod.

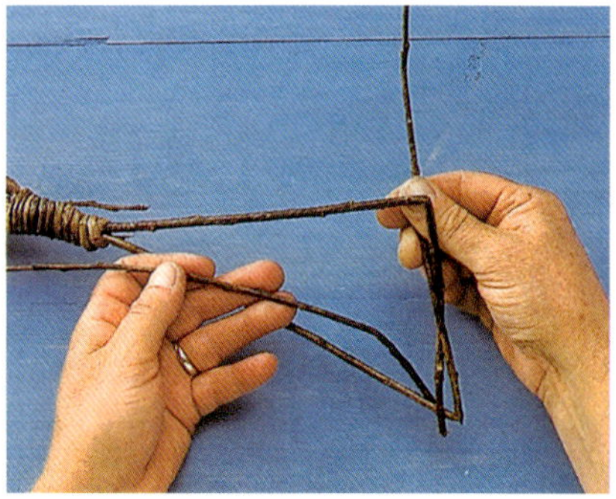

6 Kink the 2 thin tips to make the tail. Cross them in a loose knot and take them back in a curve, using a bodkin to thread them away into the wrap. Neatly trim all the ends against a stake.

MATERIALS AND EQUIPMENT YOU WILL NEED

4 x 1.5 m (5 ft) brown willow rods • Approximately 24 x 1.2 m (4 ft) slender willow rods: brown, buff and white • Craft knife • Bodkin • Masking tape • Secateurs (shears)

SHAKER

BOTH THE SHAPE AND COLOUR OF THIS DESIGN WERE INSPIRED BY SHAKERS THAT ORIGINATED IN VARIOUS AREAS OF AFRICA. ORIGINALLY, A GOURD WOULD HAVE BEEN USED TO MAKE THE BASE AND SMALL OBJECTS SUCH AS BEADS, STONES, GRAINS OR DRIED PULSES WOULD HAVE BEEN USED TO PRODUCE THE SOUND. DUE TO THE MATERIALS USED, THIS WOULD NOT BE A SUITABLE PLAYTHING FOR A BABY OR YOUNG CHILD.

1 Mark 20 evenly spaced holes around the rim of the can lid and pierce with a bradawl. File any sharp edges. Alternating the colours, thread loops of No 5 cane through adjacent holes in the lid from underneath.

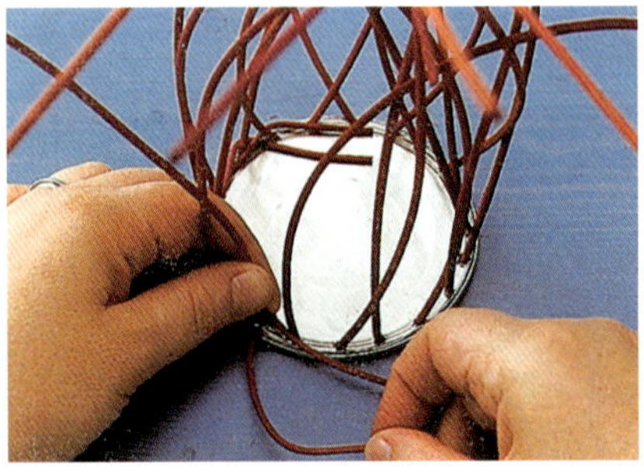

2 Take 2 strands of No 3 cane of the same colour. Lay in 2 consecutive spaces and pair for 4 rows.

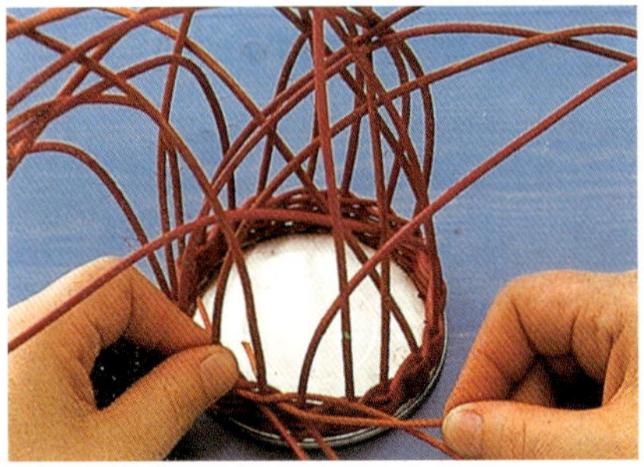

3 Change colour by joining in 2 new strands of No 3 cane and weave 4 rows. Continue pairing and changing colour every 4 rows.

4 At the start of the 4th stripe of colour, begin to curve the rattle by pushing the stakes gently inwards and weaving just a bit tighter. Put some small objects, such as beads, bells or pebbles, into the rattle.

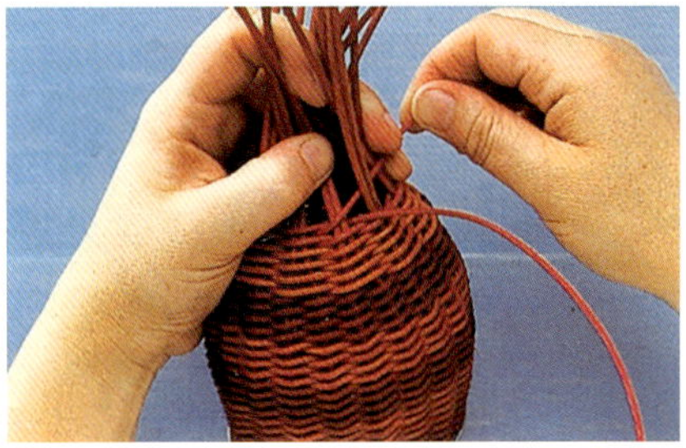

5 At the beginning of the 6th stripe begin pairing over 2 stakes of the same colour at a time. This will help to curve the work in more quickly. Choose 2 long weavers and change colour one more time. Work 4 more rows to give a total of 28 rows and 7 stripes, but don't complete pairing or cut off the long weavers.

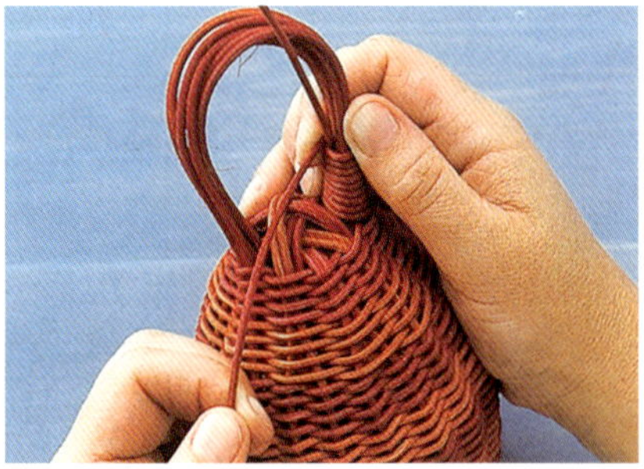

6 Divide the stakes into 4 groups: 2 pairs, 3 pairs, 2 pairs and 3 pairs. Bend over the 2 groups of 2 pairs that are opposite each other, to form a loop about 6–8 cm (2½–3 in) high, for the handle. Tuck the ends of the loop inside the rattle. Interweave and tuck in the remaining pairs of stakes to close over the opening. Bind the handle loop with 1 long weaver, carrying the 2nd weaver underneath the stakes. When the binding weaver runs out, swap over with the 2nd weaver and finish the binding, carrying the end of the 1st weaver in with the handle loop. Tuck all the ends inside the rattle.

MATERIALS AND EQUIPMENT YOU WILL NEED

PENCIL OR MARKER PEN • CAN LID, APPROXIMATELY 9 CM (3½ IN) DIAMETER • BRADAWL • METAL FILE • 10 X 60 CM (24 IN) NO 5 CANE, DYED IN 2 COLOURS, FOR THE STAKES • NO 3 CANE, DYED IN 2 COLOURS, FOR THE WEAVERS • BELLS, BEADS OR PEBBLES

Fish Mobile

This mobile can be very simple with as few as three or four fish, or it can be made much bigger to create the illusion of a whole shoal shimmering in sunlight; this one uses seven. Beads in similar colours to the fish work well, especially if they are iridescent like the ones used here. The fishing line used for tying the pieces together is available from angling shops.

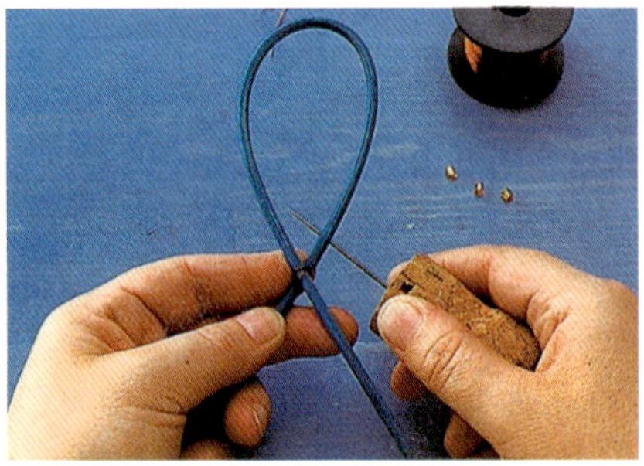

1 For each fish, tie a 36 cm (14 in) length of cane into a simple fish shape using copper wire and following the diagram and finished picture. Transfer the zigzag points on to the cane with very faint marks. Pierce the cane with a needle at the mark near the copper tie. This will be the bottom of the fish.

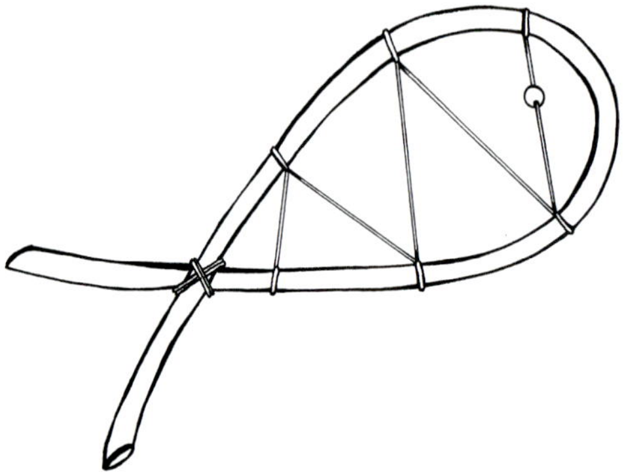

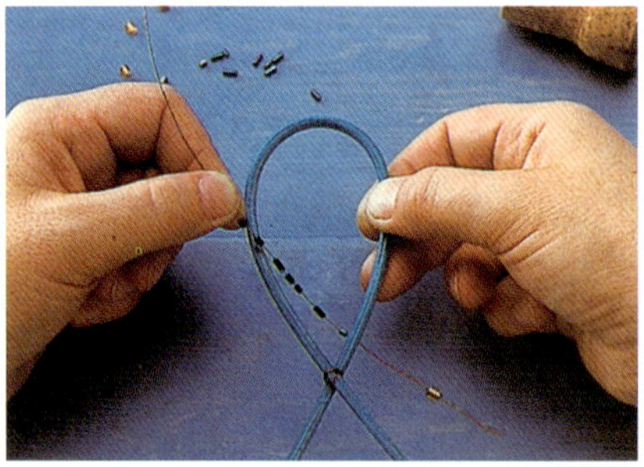

2 Thread a bead on to a 41 cm (16 in) length of copper wire and secure it with a knot. Thread the wire through the hole in the cane, then thread on enough beads to form the 1st line of the zigzag. Pierce the cane at the next mark, thread the wire through the hole and wrap it once around the cane. Add more beads for the remaining lines of zigzags.

3 At the last zigzag, thread on a contrasting bead near the top to create an eye. Thread the end of the wire through the hole and secure it with a knot.

4 Trim off the ends of cane to form the tail. Leave them a little long so you can adjust the length when you check the balance of the mobile. Attach a loop of wire with a bead threaded on it to the centre of the fish's back.

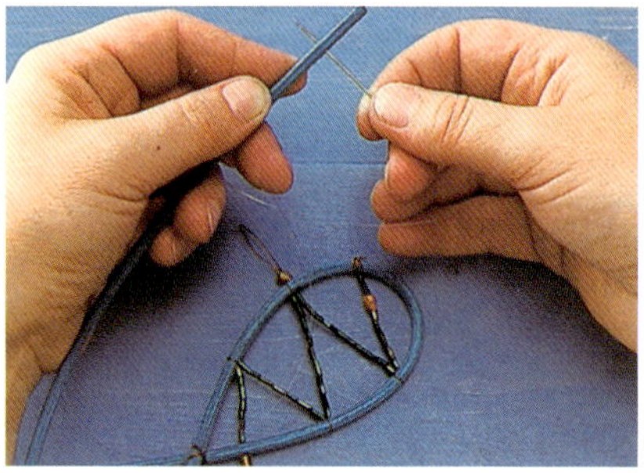

5 Tie a length of fishing line to the loop. Cut 4 lengths of cane about 25–30cm (10–12 in) long. Pierce a hole about 4 cm (1½ in) from each end of each length. Thread the fishing line through, adjust if necessary to balance and knot the line to secure.

Materials and Equipment You Will Need

No 14 cane, dyed • Side cutters • Tape measure • Copper wire • Scissors • Pencil • Needle pushed into a dense cork • Small glass beads • Fishing line

WILLOW MAT

WILLOW HAS GOOD INSULATION PROPERTIES AND IS IDEAL FOR TABLE MATS. PATTERNS CAN BE WOVEN IN USING DIFFERENT COLOURED WILLOW, AND LARGER MATS MADE FOR SERVING DISHES. THIS PROJECT WILL INTRODUCE THE BASKET-MAKER TO THE SPECIAL PROPERTIES OF WILLOW.

1 Cut 6 base sticks 23 cm (9 in) long from the thickest willow butts. Make a 3-through-3 slath and tie it in with 3 rounds of pairing. Open out the sticks into singles and continue pairing until the mat measures about 18 cm (7 in) in diameter. Join tip to tip and butt to butt. Keep the sticks evenly spaced. Thread 1 tip through the row below to prevent any unravelling. Trim all the other ends with side cutters.

2 Start a 2-rod border. Select 12 fine 90 cm (3 ft) rods and slype at the butt. With the wrong side of the mat facing, insert them 3–4 cm (1¼–1½ in) to the left of each base stick. Bend down 2 against a thumbnail, to ensure the rod bends in the correct place, 5 mm (¼ in) up from the edge of the mat. Bring the left-hand rod down behind the rod to the right and back to the front. Bring the 2nd of these down to the right behind the next stake.

3 Working on the edge of the mat, take the first of the bent down rods in front of 1 upright stake, behind the next one and back to the front.

4 Bring the left-hand upright stake down behind the next to join it and make a pair. Take the remaining single rod (the 2nd to be bent down) to the back between the 1st 2 upright stakes and back to the front, then bring the upright on the left down with it to make a pair. Repeat round the mat.

5 Take the right-hand rod of the left-hand pair and thread it under the elbow of the 1st stake to have been bent down at the start of the border.

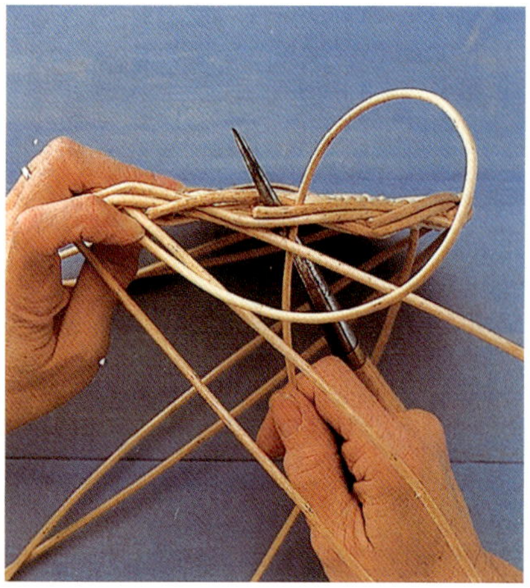

6 Bring the last upright stake down beside it. Take the right-hand stake of the last remaining pair under the next elbow, threading it from the top and positioning it to the outside of the border. Trim the border using diagonal cuts. Stand the mat on its edge and rap the border down on to the mat using a rapping iron.

MATERIALS AND EQUIPMENT YOU WILL NEED

1.2 M (4 FT) BUFF OR WHITE WILLOW RODS • TAPE MEASURE • SECATEURS (SHEARS) • BODKIN • SIDE CUTTERS • 90 CM (3 FT) WILLOW RODS • CRAFT KNIFE • RAPPING IRON

Cheese Dome

As well as looking good in the kitchen, this willow dome has a practical use: willow absorbs water when the air is humid, and retains it for a while, providing a slightly moist atmosphere for cheese storage. Flat wooden plates can be bought from kitchenware shops.

1 Cut 8 base sticks 25 cm (10 in) long from the thickest willow butts. Make a 4-through-4 slath and tie it in with 3 rounds of pairing. Open out the sticks into pairs, keeping the pairing pushed as close to the centre as possible. After 2 rows, open the base sticks into singles and continue pairing. When the diameter reaches about 10 cm (4 in), shape the base by pushing each stick individually away from you each time you pair round it. Join tip to tip and butt to butt. When the diameter reaches 20 cm (8 in), finish the pairing with tips.

2 Select 32 medium-thick 1.2 m (4 ft) rods for stakes. Slype them at the butt and insert 1 on each side of each base stick, so that the slyped surface touches the stick; this will fan them out. Push them in about 3–4 cm (1¼–1½ in). Continue pairing, pushing the stakes and remaining sections of the base sticks firmly away from you to create a curved dome. Use 4 rods for this pairing and once again finish with tips.

3 Select 32 fine rods that match well for length and thickness and begin French randing. Starting anywhere, insert the butt of 1 rod between 2 stakes, then take it in front of 1, behind 1 and back to the outside. Insert a 2nd rod in the space to the left of the 1st one then take it in front of 1, behind 1 and back to the outside. Continue in this way, putting rods in until 30 have been used.

Materials and Equipment You Will Need

1.2 m (4 ft) white willow rods • Tape measure • Secateurs (shears) • Side cutters • Bodkin • Craft knife • Rapping iron • 90 cm (3 ft) white willow rod, for the handle • Wooden plate

4 Lift the 1st 2 rods to have been inserted away from the weaving. Insert another rod under the 1st of the lifted ones then take it in front of 1, behind 1 and to the outside. Insert the last rod under the 2nd of the lifted ones then take it in front of 1, behind 1 and back to the outside. Use a rapping iron to push this row of weaving close to the dome.

5 Start a 2nd row of French randing anywhere, taking 1 weaver in front of 1 stake, behind the next and back to the outside. This creates a pair of rods in 1 space and denotes the start of the row. Use the next rod to the left in the same way. This also creates 2 rods in 1 space, but this time separated by the rod previously woven. At the end of the 2nd row (when you reach the space with 2 rods next to each other and to the outside), move up the top of the 2 rods and use the longer one, taking it in front of 1 stake, behind the next and back to the outside.

6 Rap down this row of weaving. Continue French randing until the rods are used up, rapping down at intervals. Leave the tips on the outside.

7 Work 3-rod waling above the French randing. This is started and finished with 3 tips, with a butt to butt join where necessary, the ends being trimmed to rest against stakes both inside and outside. Start a 3-rod border. Bend down 3rods against a thumbnail or bodkin, about 5 mm (¼ in) up from the weaving. Bring the left-hand rod down behind 1 upright stake. Bring the next stake to the right down in the same way, then a 3rd.

8 Take the left-hand of the 3 horizontal stakes in front of 1 upright, behind the next, then to the outside, keeping a finger inside to ensure the 1st one is not too tight. Bring the left-hand upright down beside it. Repeat this sequence until you have 3 pairs of stakes.

9 Take the right-hand rod of the left-hand pair in front of 1 upright, behind the next then to the outside. Bring an upright down beside it and repeat this sequence until you reach the beginning. Stroke the right-hand rod of the left-hand pair with your fingers to make it more pliable, then take it in front of the remaining upright, under the elbow of the 1st stake to have been turned down, threading it from the outside to the inside. Bring the upright down into the same space.

10 Continue with the remaining right-hand stakes of each pair, threading the 1st under an elbow and the 1 rod outside it, and threading the 2nd under an elbow and the 2 rods outside it. Trim the border rods with diagonal cuts using side cutters or secateurs (shears).

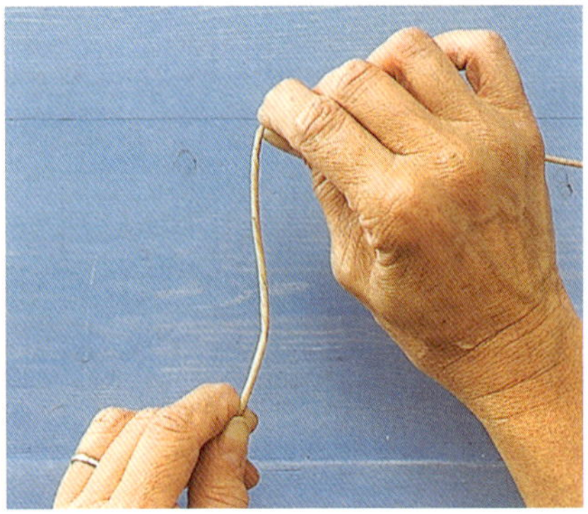

11 To make the handle, slype the butt of a perfect thin 90 cm (3 ft) rod. Using a bodkin, make a hole just outside the 3 rows which tie in the slath tie in the centre of the dome and push the butt through until about 10 cm (2 in) protrudes inside the dome. Bend the rod where it will go into the dome. Twist the rod to break the fibres: hold the rod loosely with your left hand, gripping the tip between the thumb and first finger of your right hand, and turn the rod anticlockwise (counterclockwise) with your right hand and a circular movement of the wrist and elbow. Practise this movement to get it right. Kinks will occur in the rod if the left hand tightens on the rod. Twist the whole rod; once it is twisted, you can let go and twist as you need to.

12 Using a bodkin, make a matching hole on the opposite side of the slath. Working with the butt of the rod on the right of the dome as you hold it, twist the 1st 20 cm (8 in) and push it through the hole, leaving a loop 2–3 cm (¾–1¼ in) high to create the handle. Make another hole 1 base stick towards you on the same side of the dome. Twist the handle rod underneath and pull it up, catching its own butt underneath this loop. Take it under the 1st loop and wind it round 2½ times, pulling hard to distort the 1st loop and form a rope. Keep the part of the rope you are working with twisted. Take the rod down through yet another hole, made on the right side of the handle, on the side away from you. Bring it up near you and wind it, still twisted, back to the left. Take it to the underside of the dome on the far side of the handle and cut it off underneath, leaving about 5 mm (¼ in) protruding. Shape the handle loop into a regular semi-circle.

Wall Basket

The design of this basket, with its checked pattern and flat back, makes it both decorative and useful. It will hang flush against a wall, so can be hung near a door for keys and letters, or used to hold plants. This project is suitable for experienced basket-makers.

1 Cut 6 x 30 cm (12 in) sticks from the thickest 140 cm (5 ft) white willow butts and make a 3-through-3 slath. Choose thinner rods for the weavers and tie in the slath with 2 rows of pairing, starting with tips. On the 3rd row open out the sticks into singles and weave 3 rows. Then begin to pack round 3 sticks on 2 opposite sides of the circle.

2 To pack, put the butt of 1 weaver behind the centre stick, bring it in front of the next stick to the right, wrap it behind that stick, then take it in front of the centre stick. Take it behind the next stick to the left, wrap it round to the front and take it back to the centre stick. Pair round both blocks of packing until both blocks have been enclosed at least once, then pack again as before. Continue in this way, packing and pairing, until the oval base measures approximately 20 cm x 15 cm (8 x 6 in). Trim the base sticks level with the edge of the weaving.

3 Select 24 140 cm (5 ft) white willow rods, slightly thinner than the base sticks, slype the butt end and insert one on each side of a base stick, opening a space with the bodkin if necessary. Organize the stakes so that the thicker ones are on one "long" side of the oval which will be the back of the basket. Prick up the stakes with a sharp knife. Using 4 thin white 140 cm (5 ft) rods, upsett with a 4-rod wale, in front of 2 stakes, behind 2 stakes, starting and ending with tips, and joining butt to butt and tip to tip. Weave about 8 rows, then rap down with a rapping iron.

▶

Materials and Equipment You Will Need

Side cutters • Tape measure • 140 cm (5 ft) and 90 cm (3 ft) white willow rods • Bodkin • Craft knife • Rapping iron • 90 cm (3 ft) brown (Flanders red) willow rods • Weight

4 Block weave the sides. Insert the butt ends of 12 x 90 cm (3 ft) weavers into every other space – alternating the colours brown, white – as follows. Insert a rod into a space and, working from left to right, weave it in front of 2 stakes, then behind 2. Insert the 2nd rod in the next but one space to the left and work it from left to right in front of 2 behind 2 and so on until all 12 rods are inserted. Work the weavers out to the tips for 5 rows as for French randing.

The next set of 12 weavers are inserted as before, but 1 space along to the right in order to create the colour pattern. Work a total of 6 sets of weavers of 5 rows each. Rap down to keep the weaving level.

5 Work 1 set of 4-rod waling, leaving at least 15 cm (6 in) of tips unused. Create a chequerboard effect by continuing the blocks of packing on the next level, above the 2 gaps left between the original wrapped pairs. Finally, pack above the single gap.

6 Join the 4 tips of the waling left in Step 5 and continue a further set of 4-rod waling, ending with tips. Rap down the weaving and measure the height to check that the sloping sides are even. Prick down the stakes and work a 3-rod border. Trim the stakes level with the weaving, reserving the off-cuts (scraps).

7 Slype the 24 reserved off-cuts. Turn the basket upside down and insert 1 off-cut stake each side of a stick and its 2 stakes. Lay in 3 brown willow tips and work 2 rows of 3-rod waling, ending with tips. Work a 3-rod border with the off-cut stakes. Trim off all ends. Prick down these off-cuts and work 1 set of waling. Rap down the weaving, then work another 3-rod border with brown willow. Trim off all the ends.

VASE

THE FUNCTION OF THIS VASE IS PRIMARILY DECORATIVE. IT WOULD LOOK BEST IN A SIMPLE SETTING: LEAVE IT EMPTY OR USE TO HOLD A FEW DRIED LOTUS FLOWER SEEDPODS, WHICH WOULD ECHO ITS SHAPE. PLAIN CANE OR CANE DYED IN A CLOSELY TONING COLOUR WILL ENHANCE THE TEXTURE OF THE WEAVE.

1 Make a 4-through-3 slath from the No 14 cane and weave a base 22 cm (8 in) diameter using the No 5 cane which is the same colour as the sticks. Stake up the base with 30 stakes of No 8 cane, inserting the 2 extra stakes where there are slightly wider gaps between the sticks.

2 Using the No 5 weavers which have been dyed the same colour as the sticks, upsett with 5 rows of 4-rod waling, holding the stakes at right angles to the base. Insert the bye-stakes – 2 to the right of each stake.

3 Select 2 No 5 weavers, 1 of each of the toning colours. In order to avoid a "lumpy" start, stagger the beginning of the side weaving by laying in 1 of the weavers behind a stake. Weave it in front of 3 stakes, then behind 2 stakes and to the front.

4 Lay in the 2nd weaver, on top of the 1st, behind the stake that the 1st weaver comes to the front of. Continue weaving in front of 3, behind 2, keeping the pair of weavers in a "ribbon" formation.

MATERIALS AND EQUIPMENT YOU WILL NEED

7 x 28 cm (11 in) lengths No 14 centre cane, dyed • Bodkin • No 5 centre cane, for the base and side weavers, dyed in 3 colours, including 1 the same colour as the base • 30 x 107 cm (42 in) lengths No 8 centre cane, dyed the same colour as the sticks • String • Side cutters • 60 x 43cm (17 in) lengths No 8 centre cane for the bye-stakes, dyed the same colour as the sticks • Round-nosed pliers

5 At the end of the 1st, and subsequent 7, rows, take the weavers behind 3, instead of behind 2 (this moves the weaving 1 space to the right to produce the spiralling pattern). Continue weaving up the sides. When you have worked 8 rows, change the direction of the spiral by weaving behind 1 stake at the end of the 8th and following 7 rows, instead of behind 3.

6 At the end of the next 7 rows, change the direction of the spiral again by weaving behind 3 at the end of the row, then reverting back to weave in front of 3, behind 2, and so on, up the sides of the basket to a height of around 30 cm (12 in). This weave, often known as rib-randing, tends to pull the sides of a basket inwards. So allow this to happen, but not too fast – the diameter at the top of the basket, when it has reached 30 cm (12 in) should be around 14–15 cm (5½–6 in).

7 Complete the side weaving. Stagger the ends of the weavers by working the bottom 1 of the 2 in front of 3, behind 2. Leave the ends of the weavers on the inside. Lay in 4 No 5 weavers (the same colour as the stakes) away from the ending of the side weaving, and work 2 rows of 4-rod waling. Complete the waling.

8 Soak and pinch down the stakes using round-nosed pliers, so that they can lie at right-angles to the sides. With the inside of the basket facing towards you, insert 3 No 5 weavers (the same colour as the sticks) down into the 4-rod waling, to the left of 3 consecutive stakes. Keeping the inside of the basket facing towards you, work a 3-rod wale from right to left and with no step-up. Be careful to avoid an ugly gap between the rows of waling at the point where the stakes bend outwards.

9 Concentrate on holding the stakes down at right angles to the sides, using the waling to hold them in place. When the rim measures about 5 cm (2 in) finish the waling above where it started by taking the ends of the weavers to the underside of the rim. Trim off the bye-stakes level with the waling.

10 With the basket on its side, and the top of the rim facing you, work a 4-rod border. Finally, in order to take the ends of the stakes to the underside of the rim, and to strengthen the border, work a simple follow-on border. With the top rim facing upwards, take each stake under the 2 stakes to its right, then thread it down to the underside of the rim between the border and the 3-rod waling. Use spacers at the 1st 2 stages to facilitate threading away the final stakes in sequence.

SPIRAL-PATTERNED BASKET

THIS PROJECT IS IDEAL FOR PERFECTING SHAPE CONTROL. IT ALSO USES ONE OF THE PATTERN VARIATIONS POSSIBLE WITH 3-ROD WALING, PRODUCING A SPIRAL WHICH ENHANCES THE CURVE OF THE BASKET. THE 4-ROD BORDER WITH A 3-ROD FOLLOW-ON BORDER GIVES A RIGID EDGE BY WHICH IT CAN BE PICKED UP.

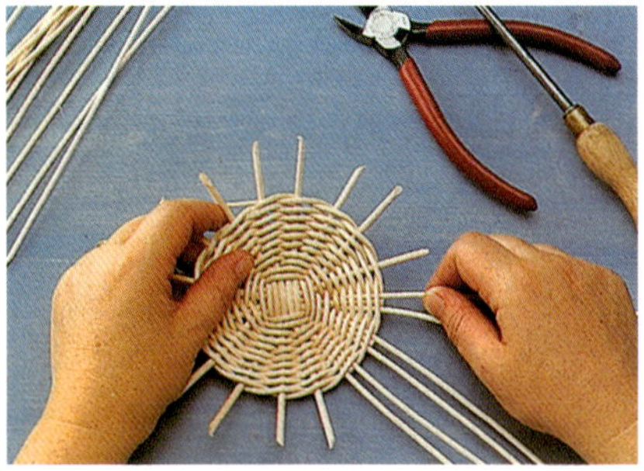

1 Cut 8 x 15 cm (6 in) sticks from the No 10 cane and make a 4-through-4 slath. Weave a 9 cm (3½ in) diameter base using natural No 5 cane. Cut 32 x 54 cm (21 in) stakes from the No 8 cane. With the dome facing away from you, insert the stakes.

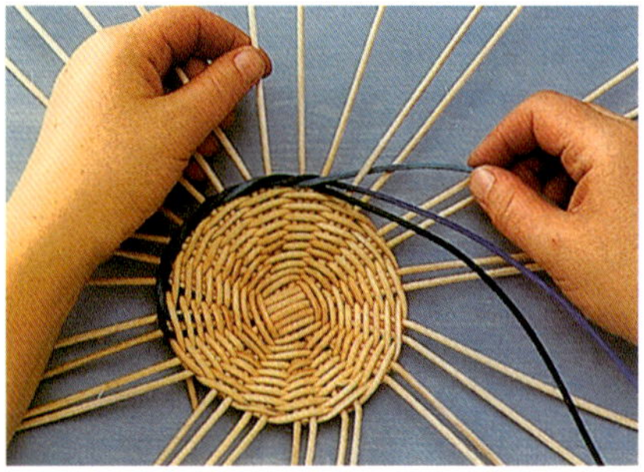

2 Keeping the dome facing away from you, insert 3 weavers (1 of each colour) to the left of 3 consecutive stakes and begin working a 3-rod wale. The colour pattern of this weave creates a spiral, so it is not necessary to work a step-up at the end of each row as this would produce a break in the pattern.

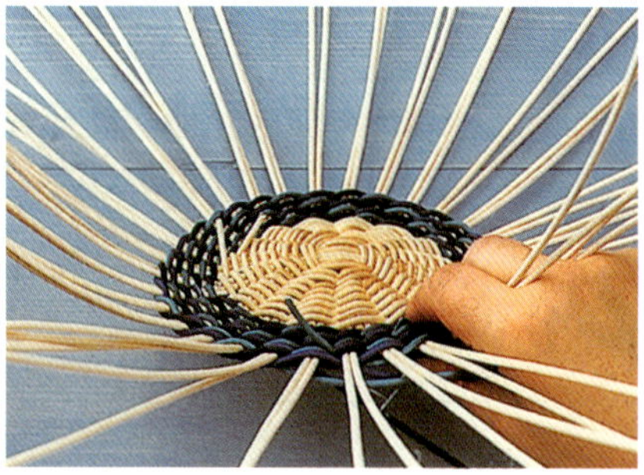

3 After 2 or 3 rows, begin pushing the stakes away from you while weaving in order to begin creating the gently curved sides of the basket. After 5 or 6 rows, cut 32 x 20 cm (8 in) No 8 cane and insert a bye-stake to the right of each stake.

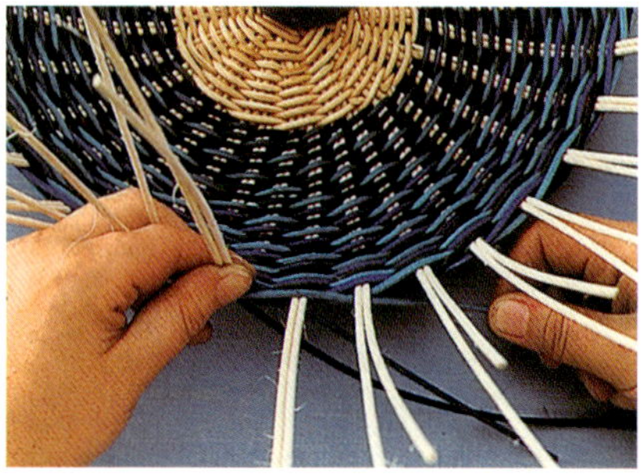

4 Continue weaving and shaping the basket with a gentle curve, placing it on its base with a weight on top when the shape allows. Complete the waling after 25 rows. At this point the basket should be approximately 27 cm (10½ in) across and 7 cm (2¾ in) high.

5 Lay 3 natural weavers into 3 consecutive spaces, and mark the stake to the left of the 1st weaver with string. Work 3 rows of 3-rod waling, working a step-up at the end of each row, and complete.

6 Trim the bye-stakes. Soak the stakes, pinch them sideways using round-nosed pliers, then work a 4-rod border. Briefly re-soak the remaining stake ends and, holding the basket on its side, work a strengthening follow-on border: a 3-rod border. Because this is a follow-on border the stakes will not be standing upright, so it is necessary to pull them back towards the left into an upright position as they are worked. Keep the border as flat as possible to avoid a gap between the 2 borders. The process of completing the follow-on 3-rod border is the same as for a normal 3-rod border, but it does look slightly different.

MATERIALS AND EQUIPMENT YOU WILL NEED

NO 10 CANE, NATURAL, FOR THE STICKS • SIDE CUTTERS • BODKIN • NO 5 CANE, NATURAL AND DYED IN 3 COLOURS, FOR THE WEAVERS • NO 8 CANE, NATURAL, FOR THE STAKES AND BYE-STAKES • WEIGHT • STRING • ROUND-NOSED PLIERS • VARNISH AND BRUSH

CHRISTMAS DOOR DECORATION

THIS CHARMING WOVEN CHRISTMAS TREE CAN BE USED ON THE FRONT DOOR IN PLACE OF A WREATH. BY VARYING THE SCALE, YOU CAN MAKE SMALLER VERSIONS FOR HANGING ON A REAL TREE OR AS FESTIVE ROOM DECORATIONS.

THE PLAITED (BRAIDED) STRAND USED TO TRIM THE BOTTOM EDGE OF THE TREE IS MADE OF DRIED THEN DAMPENED CROCOSMIA LEAVES, OVERLAPPED AS THEY ARE PLAITED. USE NATURAL STRING OR SEAGRASS IN PLACE OF THE LEAVES.

1 Bend over one-third of the tip end of 2 x 1.5 m (5 ft) thick brown willow rod. Place 1 tip inside the other to make an inverted doubled V shape. Select a 90 cm (3 ft) brown willow rod and weave a figure of eight for 8 rows around the inverted V-shape, starting with the tip and leaving enough to catch into the weaving. Keep the outside rods straight and the angle at the top constant as you work.

2 Join in a new weaver, butt to butt. Place the new end opposite the old one. Weave 2 more rows.

3 Cut a 90 cm (3 ft) length from the thick end of 2 x 1.5 m (5 ft) brown willow rods. Slype the butts and push them into the gaps next to the outside stakes. Continue to weave, working in and out of all the rods, to 18 cm (7 in). Join ends tip to tip and butt to butt. End with a tip tucked back into the weave.

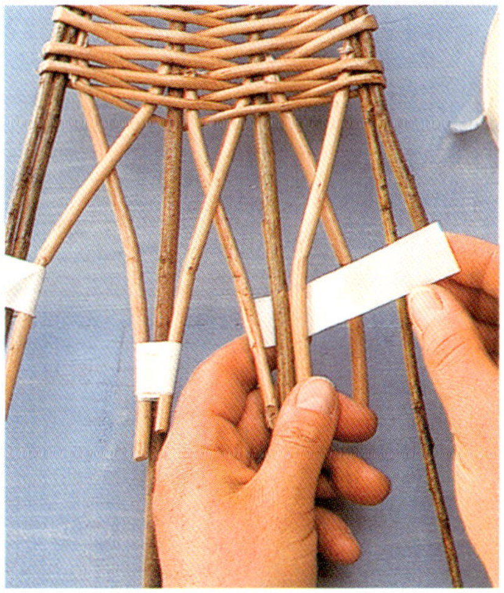

4 Cut 6 short thick ends 15 cm (6 in) long from 1.2 m (4 ft) buff rods and push them in, 1 on each side of the centre stakes and 1 inside each of the doubled outer stake. Kink them at the base of the weaving, cross them right over left and kink them again where they meet the stakes. Tape the crosses in place.

MATERIALS AND EQUIPMENT YOU WILL NEED

4 x 1.5 m (5 ft) thick brown willow rods • Mixed handful of 90 cm (3 ft) and 1.2 m (4 ft) buff and brown willow rods • Secateurs (shears) • Craft knife • Masking tape • 90 cm (3 ft) white willow rod • 1.80 m (6 ft) 3-strand plait (braid) of leaves, string or seagrass • Bodkin

5 Kink a 1.2 m (4 ft) brown willow rod so that the tip position is slightly longer than the width at the point where the crosses touch the stakes. Loop it round the left-hand side stakes and pair for the 1st row, then rand using brown and buff willow. Finish weaving after about 25 rows and join in the plaited (braided) strand.

6 To finish off the bottom edge of the tree, kink the thickest of the outside rods across to the other side, weaving it in front of and behind the stakes between. Kink it again just before the outside rod and cut a slype 5 cm (2 in) further on. Push the end into the weaving alongside the right-hand outer stake to secure. Trim the remaining right- and left-hand stakes level with the bottom of the weaving.

7 Weave the trunk of the tree over the 2 remaining stakes. Tuck a rod into the weaving then work backwards and forwards. Weave in a 2nd rod. Finish off by kinking and slyping 1 outside rod as for the base of the tree. Trim off all the ends of the weavers to lie over a stake and trim off the remaining stakes level.

8 To make the star, make 7 kinks at 2.5 cm (1 in) intervals in the white willow rod, starting 13 cm (5 in) from the tip. Starting from the kink closest to the thicker end, bend the rod round by the tip end to cross over the main rod.

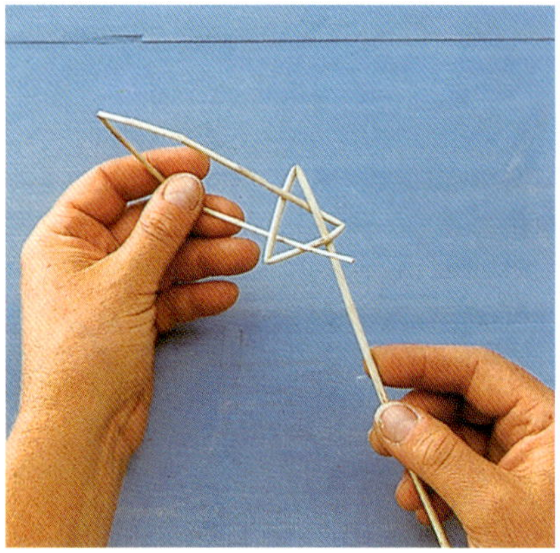

9 Make a figure 4 then take the tip end over and under itself twice and back to the start. This should make a 5-pointed star.

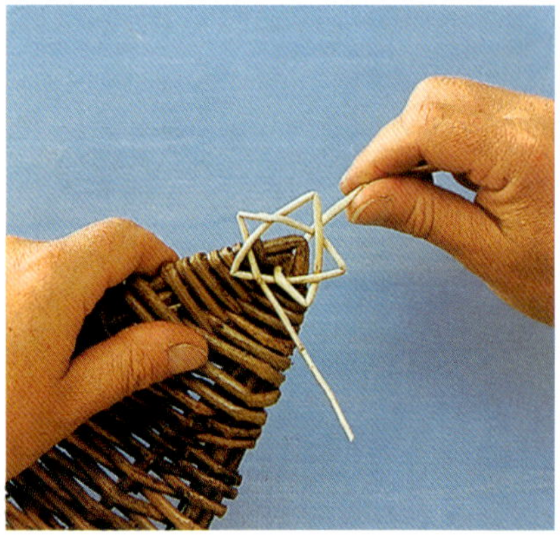

10 Attach the star to the top of the tree by threading the butt end of the rod through the weaving. Use a bodkin to make a space and follow the course of the weaving for a turn or two before cutting off the end. Trim off the tip end of the star.

TRAY

THIS PROJECT COMBINES THE PRACTICALITY OF A WOODEN TRAY WITH A CONTEMPORARY APPROACH TO ITS DESIGN. IT IS IMPORTANT TO VARNISH THE BASE BEFORE BEGINNING TO WEAVE, TO PREVENT THE WOOD FROM WARPING. HANDLES WERE CREATED FROM ROWS OF COLOURED WOODEN BEADS.

1 Cut an oval, 40 cm (16 in) long and 30 cm (12 in) wide from the plywood. Drill 60 evenly spaced holes, 6 mm (¼ in) in from the outside edge. Sand off the edges a little. Paint the base, followed by 2 coats of varnish. Cut 60 x 63 cm (25 in) stakes from the natural No 10 cane. Thread 13 cm (5 in) of the first dozen or so stakes through adjacent holes.

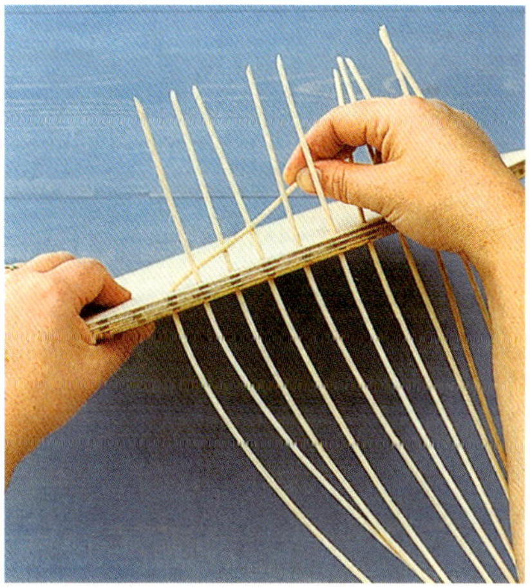

2 Working anti-clockwise (counter-clockwise), begin a foot-trac border. Take the left-hand stake down behind the stake immediately to its right, then in front of the 2nd and 3rd stakes, and finally to lie behind the 4th stake to the right.

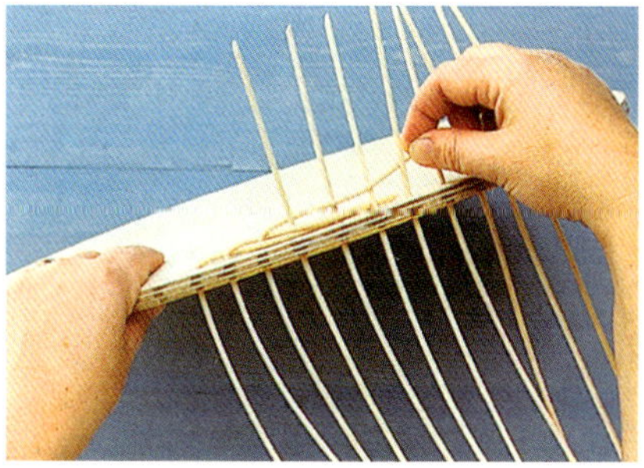

3 Adding 12 or so new stakes at a time, and always beginning with the left-hand upright, continue the foot-trac sequence: "behind 1 in front of 2 behind 1".

4 Loosen the first 3 stakes worked by pushing them up from underneath. Complete the foot-trac by keeping to the sequence. Where necessary to maintain the pattern, thread stakes under the elbows of stakes previously brought down.

5 Thread away the final upright, keeping to the same sequence. Push and pull the stakes a little if necessary to tighten and even up the foot-trac so that the tray will sit evenly on a table.

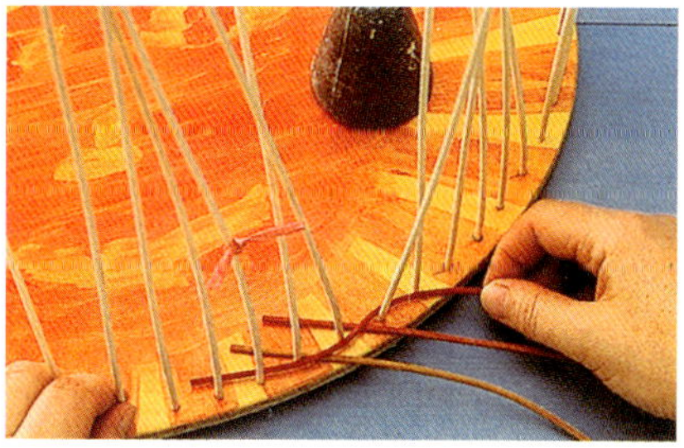

6 Turn the tray over and place a weight on it. Starting on one of the "long" sides, lay in 3 No 5 weavers, 1 of each colour, between consecutive stakes. Mark the step-up – the stake to the left of the left-hand weaver – with string, then work 3 rows of 3-rod waling, stepping-up at the end of each row. Do not complete waling. ▶

MATERIALS AND EQUIPMENT YOU WILL NEED

PENCIL • BIRCH PLYWOOD • RULER OR TAPE MEASURE • SAW • DRILL AND DRILL BIT, FOR HOLES LARGE ENOUGH TO THREAD NO 10 CANE • SANDPAPER • ARTIST'S PAINTBRUSHES • ACRYLIC PAINTS • POLYURETHANE VARNISH AND BRUSH • SIDE CUTTERS • NO 10 CANE, NATURAL AND DYED, FOR THE STAKES AND BYE-STAKES • WEIGHT • NO 5 CANE, DYED IN 3 COLOURS, FOR THE WEAVERS • STRING • BEADS, TO THREAD ON TO THE NO 10 CANE • BODKIN • ROUND-NOSED PLIERS

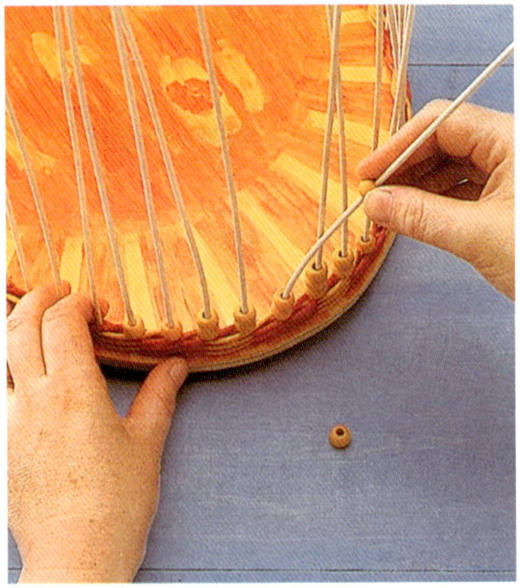

7 Thread the beads on to stakes at each end of the tray. Refer to the finished photograph for the position and arrangement of the beads.

8 Cut 60 x 48 cm (19 in) bye-stakes from the dyed No 10 cane. Insert a bye-stake to the right of every stake that does not have beads. Push them right down to the bottom of the weaving.

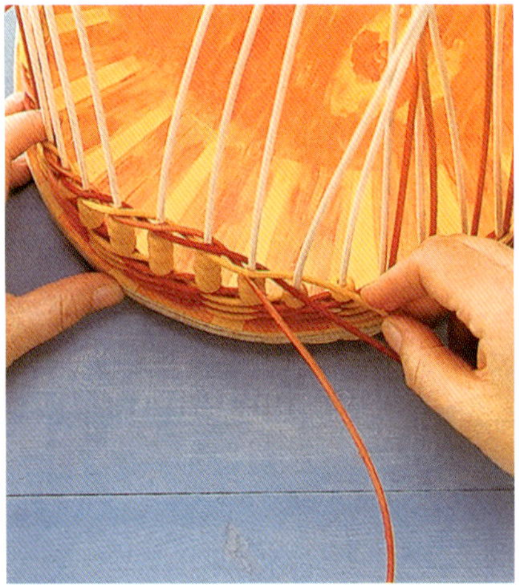

9 Pick up the 3 waling weavers and work another 3 rows, being careful to keep the weaving even when working over the beads. Complete the waling.

10 Insert the remaining bye-stakes to the right of the stakes with beads – they will only go down as far as the beads. Then cut off every other stake and its bye-stake close to the weaving.

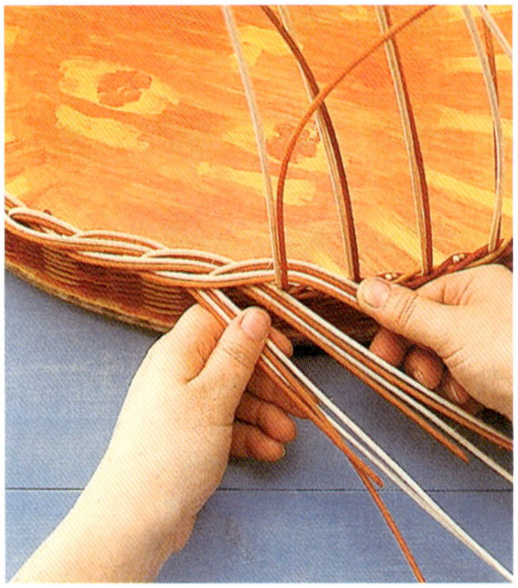

11 Work a 3-rod border, keeping the stakes and bye-stakes as one, taking care not to twist the stakes and keeping them lying flat and close together.

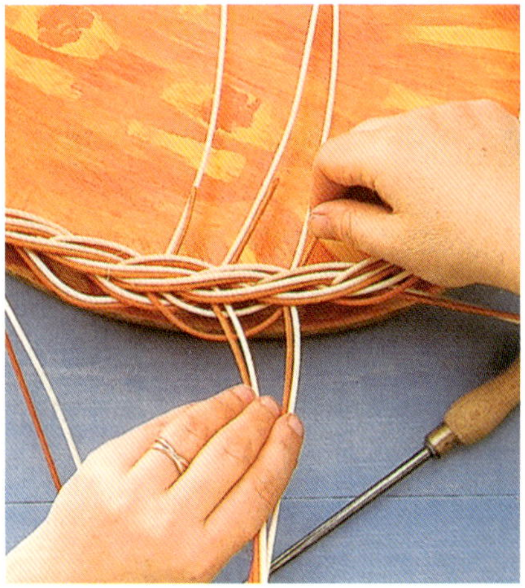

12 Work a simple follow-on border. Take a pair of stakes under the 2 pairs to the right. Thread this pair to the inside, between the weaving and the border. It will go into the same space that the right-hand pair it is going under comes out of. Trim off all the ends.

SHOPPING BASKET

SHOPPING BASKETS COME IN MANY SHAPES AND SIZES. THE SHAPE OF THIS ONE IS REMINISCENT OF THE "BOUIRRICOU", WHICH WAS DESIGNED FOR GATHERING POTATOES. ITS OVAL SHAPE AND LOW HANDLE MAKE IT EXTREMELY COMFORTABLE TO CARRY. THE RICH AND VIBRANT COLOUR SCHEME OF THIS BASKET, TOGETHER WITH ITS SMALLISH SIZE, MEAN IT COULD DOUBLE AS A FASHION ACCESSORY.

1 Cut 9 x 32 cm (12½ in) sticks from No 14 cane and make a 5-through-4 slath by threading 5 sticks through 4 to produce a slightly oval shape. Tie in with 2 rows of pairing, using orange No 5 cane. On the 3rd row open out the sticks as follows: the 2 groups of 4 into pairs, and the 2 groups of 5 into a pair, a single and a pair. Keep the central, single, stick straight. On the 5th row open the sticks out to singles.

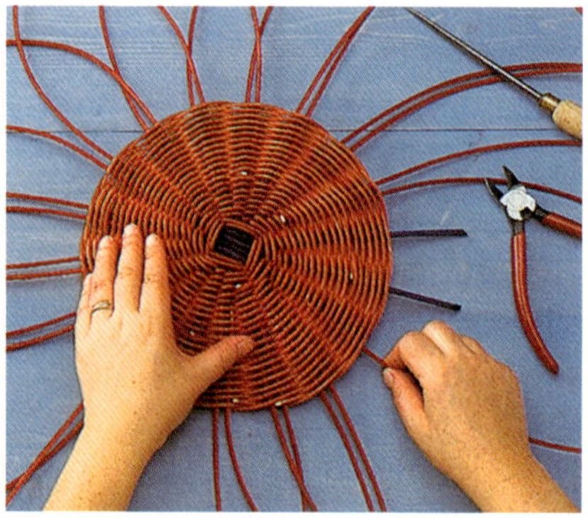

2 Weave a slightly domed base 22 cm (9 in) across. Keep the central stick straight: it will, in effect, divide the oval in half. Cut 36 x 60 cm (24 in) stakes from No 12 cane and stake-up the base.

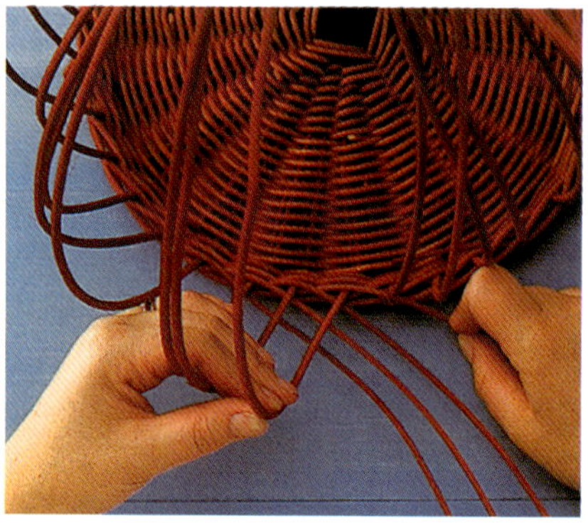

3 Continue upsetting the basket with 5 rows of 4-rod waling with red No 8 weavers, stepping-up at the end of each row. Complete the waling. Pinch and bend up the stakes, tying them into a bundle about 30 cm (12 in) above the base. Complete the 4-rod waling.

4 Cut 36 × 22 cm (9 in) bye-stakes from the No 12 cane and insert. Using 3 strands – red, orange, purple – of No 5 cane, begin working 30 rows of 3-rod waling, starting on the opposite side to where the 4-rod waling ends. Work a step-up at the end of each row.

5 After about 10–12 rows, insert the handle liners on opposite sides of the basket. Judge their position by eye, visualizing the handle crossing the finished basket. To emphasize the oval shape of the basket, thread a length of string through the weaving and tie it into shape.

6 Continue weaving the 30 rows, controlling the shape of the basket all the time. Complete the 3-rod waling. Lay in 4 red No 8 weavers, away from the completion point of the 3-rod waling, work 4 rows of 4-rod waling and complete. Trim off the bye-stakes, and any ends from joins etc. Soak and pinch the stakes. At this stage the top of the basket should measure about 41 x 25 cm (16 x 10 in) and the side weaving 18 cm (7 in) high.

MATERIALS AND EQUIPMENT YOU WILL NEED

SIDE CUTTERS • TAPE MEASURE • NO 14 CANE, DYED PURPLE, FOR THE STICKS • BODKIN OR BRADAWL • NO 5 CANE, DYED ORANGE, RED AND PURPLE, FOR THE WEAVERS AND THE HANDLE • NO 12 CANE, DYED RED, FOR THE STAKES AND BYE-STAKES • ROUND-NOSED PLIERS • STRING • NO 8 CANE, DYED RED, FOR THE UPSETT AND TOP WALING STRING • 2 HANDLE LINERS • 214 CM (84 IN) 10 MM HANDLE CANE, DYED RED, FOR THE BORDER CORE AND HANDLE BOW • CRAFT KNIFE • WEIGHT • VARNISH AND BRUSH

7 Soak a length of dyed handle cane the same length as the top circumference of the basket plus 25 cm (10 in). Shave down an end of the border core to give a tapered slype about 10 cm (4 in) long. Work the 1st stage of a 4-rod border by bringing down 4 stakes behind 1. Tie the shaved end of the core to a handle liner so that it lies on top of the brought down border stakes.

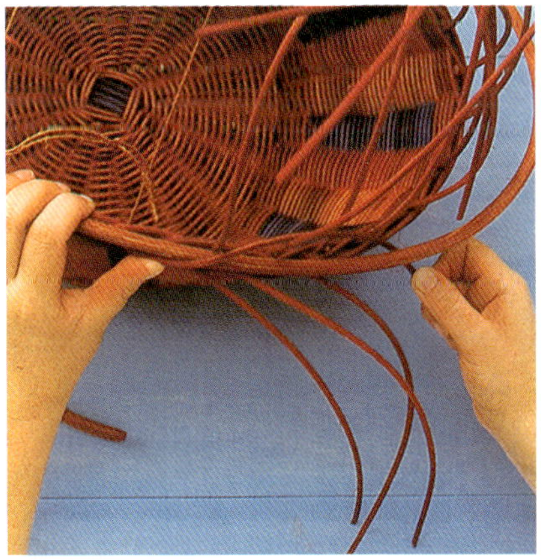

8 Continue working a 4-rod border, bringing the right-hand stake of each left-hand pair up over around the border core, in front of the 1st upright stake, behind the 2nd upright and back out to the front under the border core.

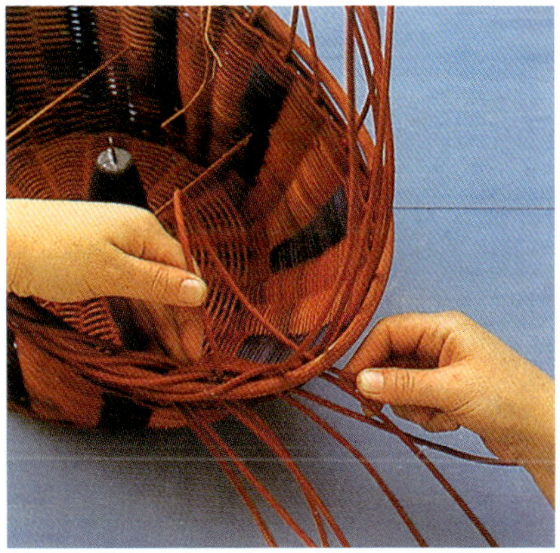

9 Bring the left-hand upright down, behind the upright stake to its right to make a pair with the brought-down right-hand stake and so on. About two-thirds of the way round the border, trim and shave down the other end of the border core so that the 2 cut edges will join up to lie neatly side by side.

10 Complete the border in the same way as for a normal 4-rod border, but working it around the core.

11 Take all the stakes to the inside by bringing each up over the core again and threading it down between the core and the 2 strands immediately behind the core. Then trim off the ends of all the border stakes so that they lie over a stake.

12 Cut a 90 cm (36 in) length of handle cane and cut a long slype on each end. Remove the handle liners and replace them with the handle bow, pushing the ends as far as possible down into the weaving. The top of the bow's curve should be about 13–15 cm (5–6 in) above the border; if necessary, remove 1 end of the bow and shave it down to reduce the length.

▶

13 Cut 5 lengths of red No 5 cane 5 times the length of the exposed part of the handle bow. With the outside of the basket facing you, thread the strands between the 3- and 4-rod waling to the left of the handle bow. Pull the strands through until there is 1½ times the length of the handle bow on the inside. Take the ends on the outside diagonally across the handle bow and wrap the handle 3 or 4 times, leaving equal-sized gaps between the wraps. Make sure the strands don't get twisted.

14 On reaching the other side, take the strands diagonally down across the handle bow and thread them to the inside between the 3- and 4-rod waling to match the first side. Bring these strands up again and, keeping them to the left of the handle bow, bring them around the front of the bow and wrap back to the other side. Leave the ends on the inside.

15 Wrap the remaining strands around the handle, filling in the gaps while taking care not to twist the strands. You may find that you only need to take 4 of these 5 strands, otherwise the underside of the handle bow may become bumpy – it is much better to have a few small gaps or "grins" on the top side – in which case, leave 1 strand behind. If, however, you find that you have a big gap on the top and underside, simply take a strand of cane a little longer than the handle bow and fill in the gap.

16 Insert a 40 cm (16 in) length of purple No 5 cane about 5–8 cm (2–3 in) down into the same space as the handle bow but to its right. Working clockwise, bind the base of the handle bow tightly 5 or 6 times.

17 Thread the end down through the binding, following the line of the handle wrapping, and thread the end to the inside. Repeat on the other side of the basket; don't worry if the 2 bindings are not identical. Trim off the ends about 4 cm (1½ in) below the binding.

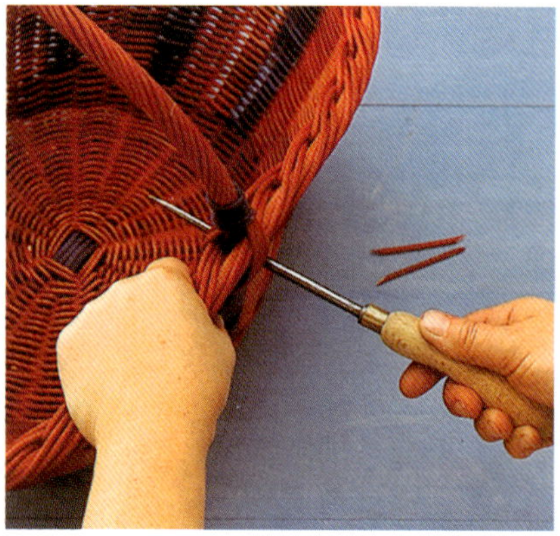

18 To secure the handle, pierce right through the handle bow with a bodkin, between the 2nd and 3rd rows of 4-rod waling. Quickly replace the bodkin with a short length of No 14 cane. Trim off both ends of the peg so that it is very slightly proud (outside) of the weaving. Finally, varnish the basket.

Lampshade

This lampshade combines two weaves producing different textures. The body of the shade is woven in pairing, the cane having been "random dyed" by suspending bundles of cane on a stick over the dye so that only a portion of the bundle is dyed. The bundles are then turned on the stick and dyed a second and then a third colour, producing unpredictable patterns. The cane and the chair cane for the Ti-band twining have been dyed in one of the colours used for the random dyeing, which gives the chair cane a mottled effect. Ti-band twining is a technique which works well combined with pairing to create the top and bottom borders of the shade.

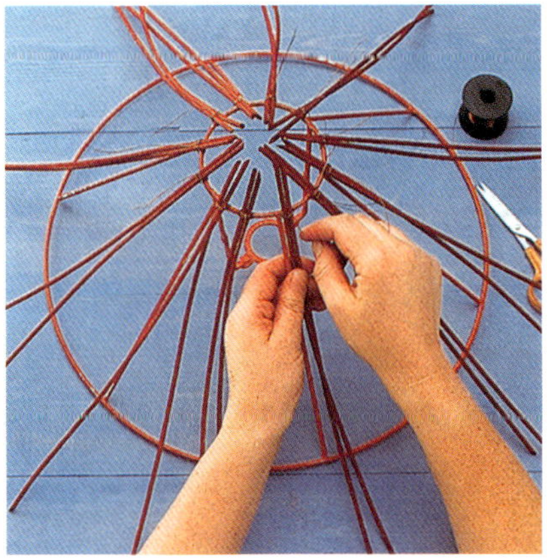

1 Cut 48 x 28 cm (11 in) stakes from No 10 cane. Using the copper wire, temporarily bind pairs of stakes to the top ring of the lampshade: 1 pair with a stake placed on either side of the vertical metal "stakes" of the lampshade, and another pair between each metal "stake".

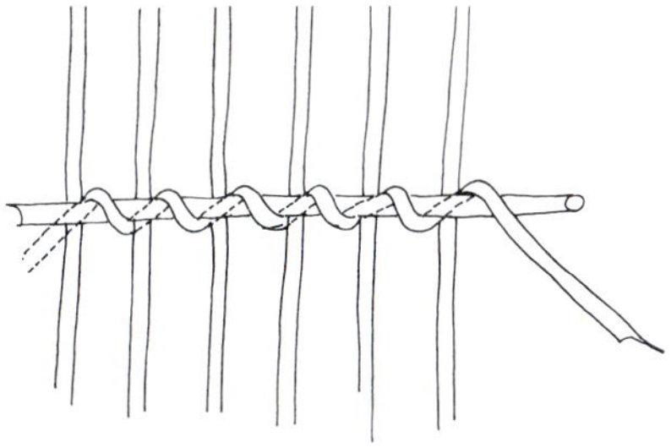

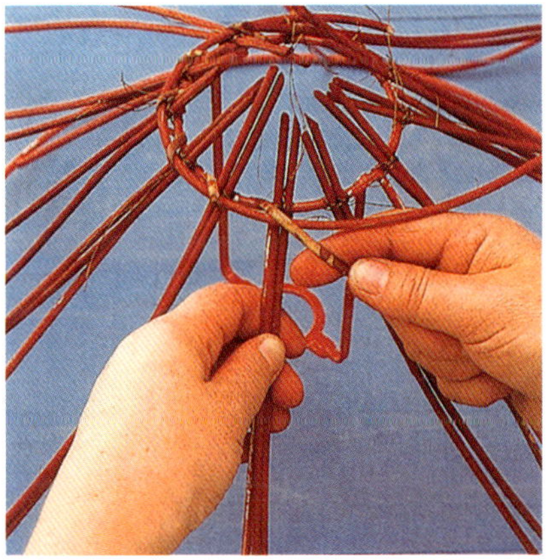

2 Push 1 end of a length of chair cane through 1 of the wire ties to secure it. With the frame in an upright position, hold a length of No 10 cane against the top ring of the frame, with the end on the left. Working anticlockwise (counter-clockwise), wrap the chair cane around the cane and the top ring to attach the cane to the outside of the top ring. Wrap diagonally down over each pair of stakes from top left to bottom right, then take the chair cane up diagonally behind the top ring and cane.

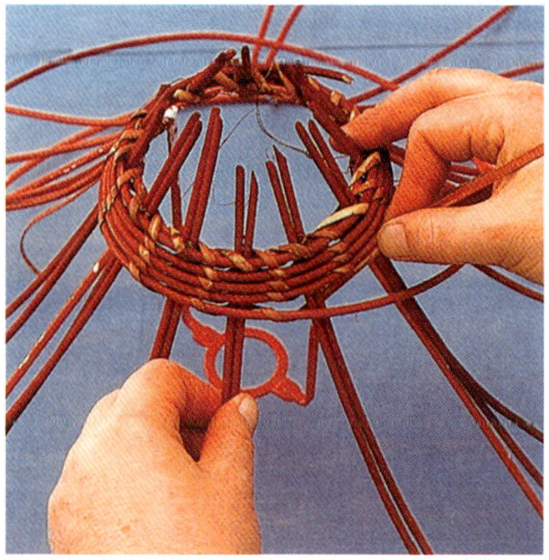

3 Continue wrapping over both the top ring and cane for a 2nd round, this time positioning the wraps between the existing wraps so that the chair cane travels behind the metal "stakes". For the 3rd round, start coiling the No 10 cane downwards around the frame. Secure it to the frame with ti-band twining: wrap the chair cane behind the stakes, diagonally from bottom left to top right, then around the front of the cane, this time working from top left to bottom right. Work 5 rows of ti-band twining (see the diagram), finishing below where you started. Temporarily secure the ends, leaving about 15 cm (6 in) of each to thread away later. ▶

Materials and Equipment You Will Need

Tape measure • Side cutters • No 10 cane, dyed • Enamelled copper wire • Scissors • Lampshade frame, 36 cm (14 in) diameter at base • Bodkin • No 6 chair cane, dyed • No 5 cane, random dyed, for the weavers • Varnish and brush

4 Turn the frame upside down. Lay in two strands of the random dyed No 5 cane and pair for 5 or 6 rows. Insert a stake on either side of the existing pairs of stakes.

5 Continue pairing. Work over the groups of stakes that include the metal "stakes", keeping them as groups of 4, but open out alternate groups of 4 into pairs. Continue pairing until the weaving measures about 14 cm (5½ in). Complete pairing.

6 Secure another length of No 10 cane (the ends will be threaded away and trimmed neatly when the lampshade is complete) and work about 10 more rows of ti-band twining. On this block of weaving, however, make 2 wraps between the stakes.

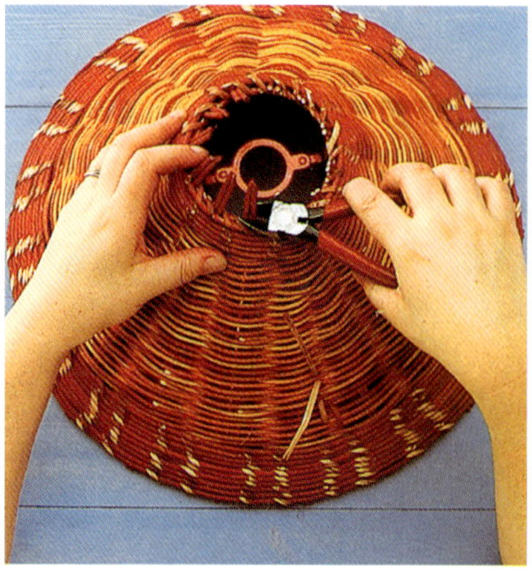

7 Remove the copper wire. Trim off the ends of the stakes about 0.5 cm (¼ in) above and below the top and bottom edges.

8 Undo the ends of chair cane where they have been temporarily secured. Thread them away securely on the inside of the lampshade so that they are not visible from the outside, taking care not to interrupt the weaving patterns. Using side cutters, neatly trim off any ends of the No 10 cane and pairing joins. Apply a coat of varnish to the outside of the lampshade and two coats to the inside. Brush the varnish in well, especially around the top and bottom edges.

IRONING BASKET

THE TRADITIONAL DESIGN FOR A LAUNDRY BASKET IS GIVEN A CONTEMPORARY FEEL HERE BY THE ADDITION OF DYED CANE. THE PATTERN OF VERTICAL STRIPES IS WORKED OVER 25 ROWS, BUT THE PATTERN COULD BE VARIED BY WORKING HORIZONTAL STRIPES, EACH STRIPE CONSISTING OF FIVE ROWS OF WEAVING. OR THE 25 ROWS COULD BE DIVIDED UP DIFFERENTLY, ADDING OR SUBTRACTING A ROW OR TWO IF NECESSARY. A SLIGHTLY MORE ADVENTUROUS PATTERN COULD BE ACHIEVED BY WORKING A BLOCK OF FIVE ROWS USING THREE COLOURS, THEN MOVING EACH COLOUR ONE SPACE TO THE RIGHT. CONTINUE FOR A TOTAL OF 25 ROWS, MOVING THE COLOURS ONE SPACE TO THE RIGHT EVERY 5 ROWS TO PRODUCE A DIAGONAL SLANT.

1 Cut 10 x 37 cm (15 in) sticks from thick butt ends of the longest thick willow rods and make a 5-through-5 slath, tie in with 2 rows of pairing, then open out each group of 5 sticks firstly into groups of 2,1,2 and then, after a further 2 rows, into singles. Continue weaving a slightly domed base to a diameter of 33 cm (13 in). Complete the pairing. Stake-up the base with 40 stakes and add 1 extra stake on opposite sides of the basket.

2 Prick-up the stakes and tie above the base. Insert 4 x 1.5 m (5 ft) rods and work a 4-rod wale halfway round the base; then insert a further 4 rods to give 2 sets of weavers. Continue working with 2 sets of weavers for a height of 4 cm (1½ in), holding the stakes out a little to give a slight outward flow. Ending with the tips, complete the waling.

3 Insert 3 dyed cane weavers, one of each colour, and mark the step-up. Work about 15 rows of 3-rod waling remembering to step-up at the end of each row. Thread a length of string through the dyed cane waling and tie the basket into an oval shape. Continue the 3-rod waling, keeping the oval shape regular, for a total of 25 rows. Complete the waling.

▶

MATERIALS AND EQUIPMENT YOU WILL NEED

BODKIN • SIDE CUTTERS • SECATEURS (SHEARS) • 20 X THICK 1.8 M (6 FT) BUFF WILLOW RODS, FOR BASE STICKS AND HANDLE BOWS • 90 OR 120 CM (3 OR 4 FT) BUFF WILLOW RODS, FOR BASE WEAVERS • 50 X 1.8 M (6 FT) BUFF WILLOW RODS, FOR STAKES • ROUND-NOSED PLIERS • 1.5 M (5 FT) BUFF WILLOW RODS, FOR TOP AND BOTTOM WALE • NO 10 CANE, DYED IN 3 COLOURS • STRING • WEIGHT • CRAFT KNIFE • VARNISH AND BRUSH

4 Lay in 4 x 1.5 m (5 ft) willow rods, work a 4-rod wale halfway around the basket, lay in 4 more rods and continue waling with 2 sets of weavers for 3 cm (1¼ in). Check that the basket is level all the way round. At this stage the top should measure 60 x 41 cm (24 x 16 in) and the height at the side 24 cm (9 ½ in). Re-soak the stakes if necessary, then prick-down and work a 4-rod behind 2 border.

5 For the border, bring down 4 rods, with each brought down behind the 2 stakes to its right. Pick up the left-hand stake, take it in front of 2 uprights to the right and behind the 3rd. Bring the left-hand upright down behind the 2 uprights to its right to make a pair. Make 4 pairs. Pick up the right-hand stake of the left-hand pair, then work it in front of 2 uprights and behind 1, bringing the left-hand upright down behind 2 to make a pair. Continue round the basket, until 2 stakes remain upright.

6 Take the right-hand stake of the left-hand pair in front of these 2 uprights. Take it behind, and then thread it to the front under the very 1st brought-down stake. Bring the left-hand upright down behind the remaining upright and thread under the same brought-down stake to make a pair.

7 Again, take the right-hand stake of the left-hand pair in front of the last upright. It is then taken in front of and threaded under the 1st brought-down stake, then behind and under the 2nd brought-down stake. Bring the final upright down to make a pair.

8 To complete, identify the 1st 4 single brought-down stakes and, using the right-hand stake of each pair, make these into pairs following the pattern of the border.

9 Cut 2 handle bows from the butt ends of 2 x 1.8 m (6 ft) thick willow rods, slype both ends of each and push each end down beside a stake, about 8 cm (3 in) into the weaving approximately 16.5 cm (6½ in) apart on either end of the basket. The top of the bow should be 7.5 cm (3 in) above the border.

10 For each handle, cut 3 lengths of dyed cane 5 times the length of the handle bow. With the outside of the basket facing you, insert these between the cane and willow waling in a "ribbon" formation, to the left of the handle bow; leave 1½ times the length of the handle bow on the inside. Bring the remaining lengths diagonally up across and then under the handle bow. Make 3 wraps, then bring the strands diagonally back down across the handle bow and thread them through the waling to match the other side.

11 Bring the strands straight up behind the willow waling, under the handle bow and wrap them back to the left-hand side, partially filling in the gap in the wrapping.

12 Pick up the other set of wrapping strands, bring them straight up behind the waling to the left of the handle bow and over around the handle bow, wrapping across to the other side, and filling in the gap. You may find that you only need 2 of the strands at this stage, in which case leave 1 behind. Leave the ends on the inside.

13 Insert a strand of dyed cane about 36 cm (14 in) long to one side of the handle bow and bind the handle with 4 or 5 wraps. Thread the end back down through the binding. Trim off the ends of the wrapping strands to about 2.5 cm (1 in) below the binding. Peg the handle at each end of the bow. Repeat the above on the other side of the handle bow. Finally, varnish the cane area of the basket.

P1

Bicycle Basket

The design of this basket makes it more versatile than most as it is easy to remove from the handle bars. The hinged handle makes the basket easy to carry for shopping. It is big enough to take a folder or two, a lunch box and a newspaper to work, college or school. If you have an old secondhand bike, you may want to brighten it up with a new coat of paint and then dye the cane in colours to match.

1 Cut 8 x 33 cm (13 in) sticks from the butt ends of 1.5 m (5 ft) willow rods and make a 4-through-4 slath. Tie in with 2 rows of pairing, open to pairs for 2 rows, then open to singles. Weave until the base measures 10 cm (4 in) in diameter. Starting with the butt end of a 1.2 m (4 ft) rod, work 2 short rows of weaving in a similar way to packing, to begin the shape for the base. Work the 1st about two-thirds round the base, leaving both ends underneath. Make the 2nd row a little shorter.

2 Work a few rows of packing: starting with the butt of a 1.2 m (4 ft) willow rod, pack about two-thirds of the way around the base, turn round a stick then weave back the other way, until all the rod is used up. Leave the tip underneath.

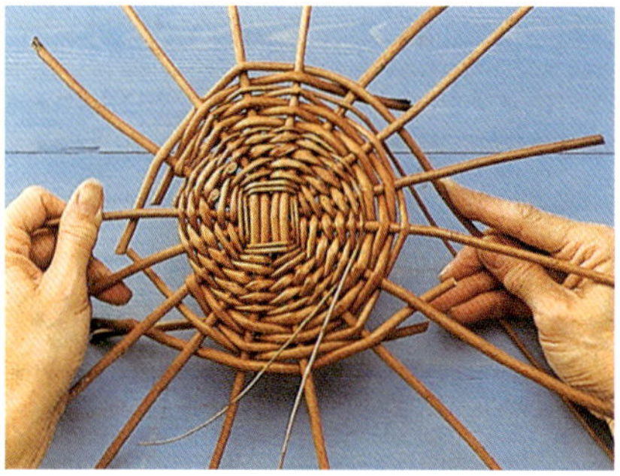

3 Work 2 more short rows of weaving on the opposite side, about ⅓ round the base; leave both ends underneath. Put in another butt, weave it further round and leave the tip underneath.

4 Continue building up the base into an oval approximately 20 x 26 cm (8 x 10½ in), with a flattish side that will go at the back of the basket.

Materials and Equipment You Will Need

1.2 and 1.5 m (4 and 5 ft) buff willow rods • Tape measure • Secateurs (shears) • Side cutters • Bodkin • Craft knife • Galvanized wire (similar to a metal coat hanger) •Wire cutters • Round-nosed pliers • No 10 cane, dyed in 3 colours • String • Weight • Rapping iron • Masking tape • Varnish and brush • 2 leather straps

5 Starting with tips, weave 2 rows of pairing round the whole base, finishing with tips, and with a butt to butt join where necessary.

6 Select 32 stakes from 1.5 m (5 ft) rods, evenly matched for thickness. Slype each on the back of the curve, and with the right side of the base facing and the slyped side uppermost, upsett with 30 stakes, pushing them in as far as possible. On each side of the basket, where the handles will be, use a bodkin to pierce the pairing weavers where they cross between 2 base sticks.

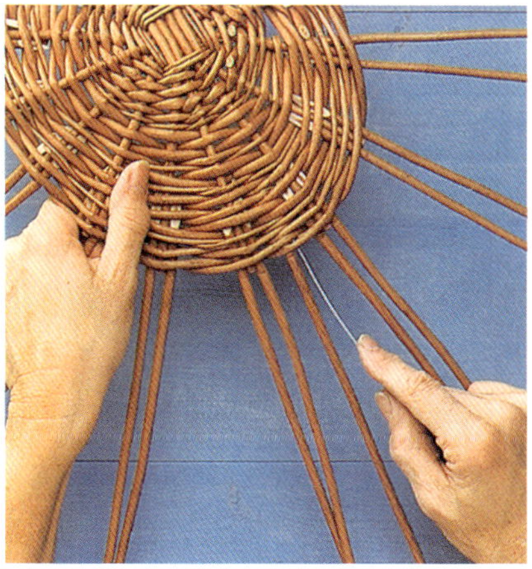

7 Insert a stake through the pierced willow on each side of the basket and then a length of wire alongside.

8 Prick up the stakes and hold them in a hoop. Upsett with a 3-rod wale, weaving over the wire and adjacent stake as one. Continue waling, joining rods butt to butt or tip to tip as necessary and rapping down hard at intervals. When the weaving is 4 cm (1½ in) high, complete waling.

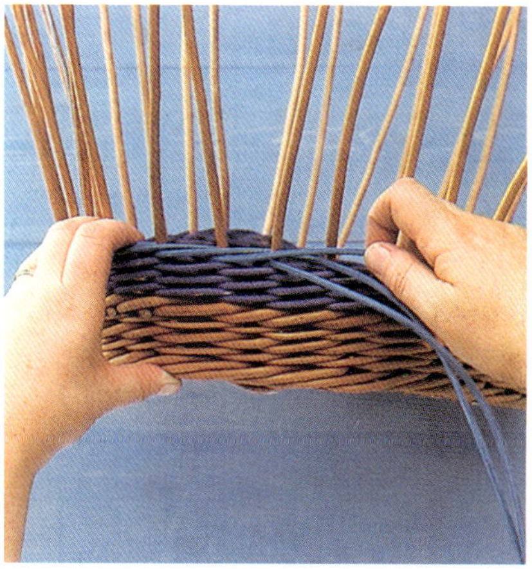

9 At the back, lay in 3 purple weavers and mark the step-up. Work 3 rows of 3-rod waling. Complete waling. At a different starting point, but towards the back of the basket, lay in another 3 blue weavers and wale for 3 more rows, remembering to step-up.

10 Continue waling, changing colour every 3 rows and keeping the starting points of each block towards the back of the basket. After 5 or 6 blocks of colour, tie the basket to increase the oval shape slightly. Continue working until you have 9 stripes. Complete the waling. ▶

11 Bend each wire down to make a loop about 4 cm (1½ in) above the level of the weaving. Starting with the tips, lay in 3 x 1.5 m (5 ft) fine willow rods. Begin a 3-rod wale joining butt to butt then ending with tips. Work around the loop and the stake it is next to, as one. Complete the waling and check the level of the basket, rapping down where necessary. The top measures roughly 46 x 27 cm (18 x 10 ½ in).

12 Work a 4-rod border as for the gathering basket, working around the 2 looped wires. Trim off ends of stakes and weavers. Cut a 200 cm (78 in) length of wire. Thread the ends through the 2 wire loops and adjust the length and shape of the wire to match the front curve of the basket's border. This will form the handle bow. There should be equal lengths of wire remaining through the loops. Take 1 of these lengths and, bending it up to form a loop which interlocks with the loop protruding from the border, wrap it around the handle bow to the other end. Repeat on the opposite side.

13 Select 8 perfect fine willow rods, 1.5 m (5 ft) long and slype the butts. Tape the ends of 4 of these to an end of the wire handle bow. Wind the rods round the wire over to the other end. Repeat at the other end, filling in the gaps from the first wrapping. Tape in several places to secure the wrapping until bindings are added. The handle should be able to move freely between an upright, carrying position and a resting position on the curve of the front border of the basket; the curve of the handle should match this front curve as accurately as possible.

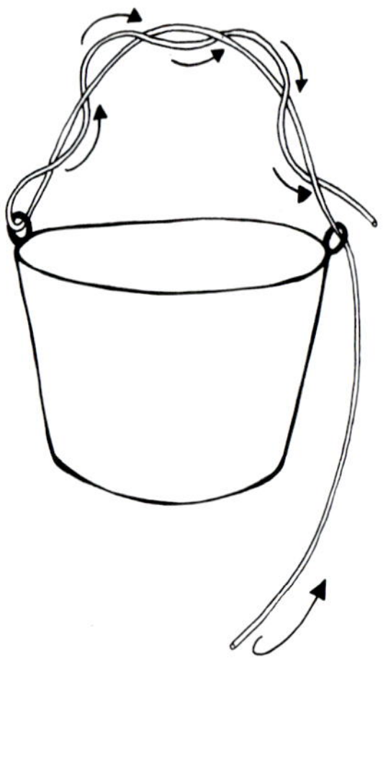

14 Bind the cane around the ends of the handle, as described in the willow fan. Remove the masking tape.

15 Trim off the ends of the binding cane, and the ends of the willow about 2.5 mm (⅛ in) from the bottom of the binding. Varnish the cane areas of the basket. Finally, thread the straps between the cane and willow waling, positioning them according to the handlebars of the bicycle the basket is to be attached to.

GATHERING BASKET

THIS SMALL BASKET IS BASED ON A TRADITIONAL DESIGN ORIGINALLY USED FOR FRUIT-PICKING AND GATHERING NUTS. IT CAN BE MADE UP IN A WIDE VARIETY OF WILLOWS AND WEAVES, AND CAN BE USED TO CONTAIN ALL KINDS OF ITEMS, FROM CLOTHES PEGS TO EGGS.

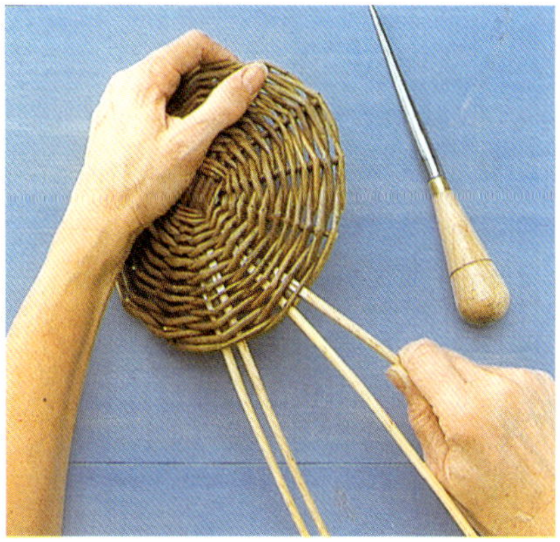

1 Cut 6 base sticks 20 cm (8 in) long from the thickest 1.2 m (4 ft) brown willow butts. Make a 3-through-3 slath and tie it in with 3 rounds of pairing. Open out the sticks into singles and continue pairing until the base measures about 15 cm (6 in) in diameter. Join butt to butt and tip to tip and keep the sticks as evenly spaced as possible. Finish the weaving with tips and thread 1 of these through the row below. After the first butt to butt join, push the base sticks slightly away from you to give the base a curve. Trim all the other ends. Slype 24 of the 1.2 m (4 ft) white willow rods on the back of the curve. Push them into the base with the cut surface uppermost, 1 each side of each base stick, using a greased bodkin to make a space if necessary.

2 Holding the base down with your forearm or a weight, place a knife blade on and parallel to the stake, about 3–4 mm (⅛ in) up from the base edge. Lift the stake with your free hand, while turning the knife through 90 degrees, then let the stake go. This gives a spreading out on the top surface of the rod only. Repeat for each stake. Pull all the stakes up and keep them upright by placing a 30 cm (12 in) diameter hoop, made from 2 tied 1.5 m (5 ft) willow rods, over them.

3 Start a 3-rod wale by inserting the tips of 3 x 1.2 m (4 ft) brown rods into the base to the left of 3 consecutive stakes. With the underside of the base towards you, bend the 3 weavers down towards you. Take the left-hand weaver in front of 2 stakes to the right and behind the 3rd. Tuck it well down to the base, between the base stick and stake if possible. Repeat with the new left-hand weaver and continue weaving. The first row should be underneath the basket, the next will come up the side and is used to set the angle of the stakes to the base. ▶

MATERIALS AND EQUIPMENT YOU WILL NEED

1.2 M (4 FT) BROWN WILLOW RODS • TAPE MEASURE • SECATEURS (SHEARS) • SIDE CUTTERS • GREASE POT • BODKIN • KNIFE • 1.2 M (4 FT) WHITE WILLOW RODS • WEIGHT • 2 X 1.5 M (5 FT) WILLOW RODS • RAPPING IRON • 20 CM (7 IN) WILLOW ROD FOR HANDLE

4 After the 1st 2 rows, push the butt end of a new rod in beside each of the 3 butts projecting to the outside to leave 5 cm (2 in) or so on the inside. New ends are inside, old ones outside. Make sure they sit side by side. Take the new left-hand rod in front of 2 stakes, behind the next, as in step 3. Work each new rod in sequence and continue waling until you reach the tips of the rods. Rap down the waling to close the rows of weaving.

5 Work the sides of the basket in English randing. Select 24 weavers of 1.2m (4 ft) white willow for the sides of the basket and start randing. Starting anywhere, put a butt in from the right to sit behind a stake and project inside about 1 cm (½ in) to the left of it. With the first 2 fingers of your left hand behind the next stake to the right, holding it at the angle you want, push the weaver in with your left thumb and bring it out again with your right hand. Continue weaving this way, in front of 1 stake, behind 1, to complete 1 round, so the tip comes out beside the butt.

6 Place the butt of a new weaver in the space to the right of the first and weave 1 round so the tip comes out with the butt as before. Continue weaving the remaining 22 rods in this way, using a rapping iron every 3 or 4 rows to close up the weaving. Rap down until the side is level all the way round. Insert 3 tips of 1.2 m (4 ft) brown willow into 3 consecutive spaces, starting anywhere, and work out to butts, join, then work back to tips, leaving them on the outside. Rap down until the top is level.

7 Starting anywhere, start a 4-rod border: first, bend 5 stakes down against a thumb nail or a bodkin, about 5 mm (¼ in) up from the top of the basket and stand them up again.

8 Take the left-hand bent stake down behind the stake to its right and out to the front. Repeat with 3 more stakes so that 4 project horizontally.

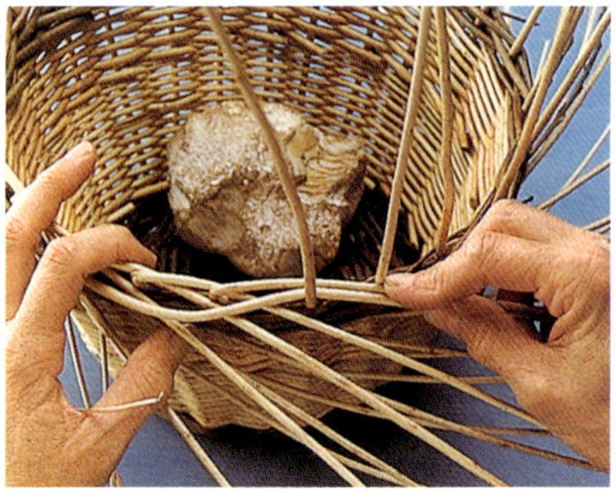

9 Take the left-hand bent stake in front of the next upright stake to the right, behind 1 and back to the front. Keep a finger inside it to ensure this stake is not too tight. Bring the left-hand upright stake down to make a pair.

10 Repeat step 9 to create pairs of horizontal stakes, until you are back at the start and there is 1 upright stake remaining. Leave the left-hand stake behind each time. Stroke the right-hand horizontal stake of the left-hand pair to soften, then thread it in front of the upright stake and behind and under the next, which is the first to have been brought down at the start of the border, threading it back to the front.

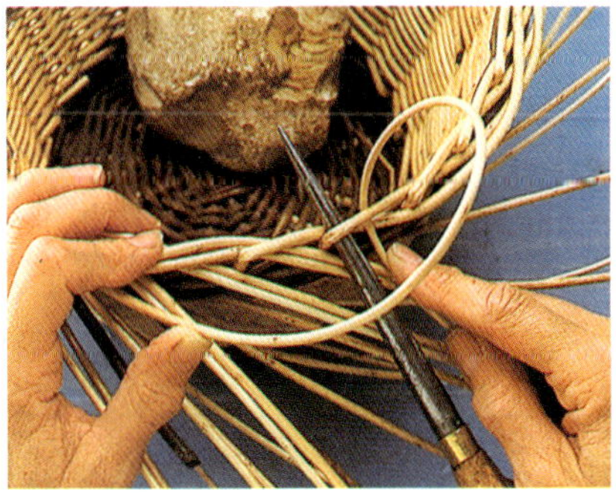

11 Bend the upright stake down and thread it through beside the stake worked in step 10, to make a pair. The right-hand horizontal stake of the new left-hand pair is threaded under the 2nd stake bent at the start of the border, from the back to the front. It lies in front of the 1st brought-down stake and touches the bent elbow of the 2nd.

12 Thread the right-hand horizontal stake of the next new left-hand pair into the equivalent position as in step 11, under the elbow of the 3rd stake to have been bent down at the beginning of the border, and under 1 rod on the outside of the border. Try to avoid kinking the stakes as you thread them away.

13 Repeat the above sequence with the right-hand horizontal stake of the new left-hand pair, threading it from behind, under the 4th stake to have been bent down at the beginning of the border and under 2 willow rods on the outside of the border. Use the right-hand stake of the last remaining pair to complete the border by threading under the next elbow and under 3 rods outside the border.

14 Pull each horizontal stake out to the left and cut it on the diagonal using secateurs. Trim the rest of the basket. You can cut the tips outside the basket wherever they seem secure. Those on the inside must be cut against an upright stake so they cannot slip through to the outside.

15 Cut a 7.5 cm (3 in) slype on the handle bow rod, on the belly of the butt of the rod. Use a bodkin to make a deep opening beside a stake and push the slyped butt down as far as you can with the slype to the inside of the basket. Bend the rod over to judge the handle height and cut the rod to length, making sure there is enough to push down on the 2nd end. Slype the inside of the thin end and insert the handle bow without kinking it, as before.

▶

16 Secure the handle at each end with a willow peg. Make a hole through the handle between the white waling and the brown top waling, large enough to take a section of willow. Insert a peg into each hole and tap it into position using a rapping iron.

17 Select 8 fine white 1.2 m (4 ft) rods, checking that they have no kinks or blemishes, and slype them at the butt. Insert 4 of them to the left of 1 end of the bow, having first made an opening with a bodkin. Push them in about 5 cm (2 in).

18 Take the rods as a group in a wide curve and, pulling them down to the right at an angle of about 45 degrees to the top of the basket, carry them under the handle bow and round it, and over and over, leaving sections of the handle uncovered. Leave the tips sitting inside the basket. Repeat on the opposite side of the basket with the 4 remaining rods. If the bow is not completely covered, you may need to add an extra rod and wind it round, probably on 1 side.

19 On each side of the basket, make a hole with the bodkin between 2 rows of top waling, just below the border, and thread each group of tips to the outside.

20 Secure the tips. Take each group up to the left, round the inside of the handle and down to the left, pulling the rods close against the handle. Make another hole on the left of the handle (seen from the outside), thread the tips through and pull tightly.

21 Twist the tips inside the basket into a rope and thread them back through to the outside through the 1st hole. Twist the tips again and take them back to the inside between 2 rows of waling in the next space between stakes to the right. Trim the ends against a stake.

WASTEPAPER BASKET

THIS STRAIGHT-SIDED CYLINDER IS ANOTHER GOOD EXERCISE IN SHAPE CONTROL. THE SIDING HAS A RICH TEXTURAL WEAVE, BUT IT WOULD BE EQUALLY EFFECTIVE IF WOVEN WITH PLAIN PAIRING AFTER THE UPSETT, WHICH WOULD PROVIDE AN EXCELLENT CANVAS FOR EXPLORING COLOUR PATTERNS ON A LARGE SURFACE. PLAN A DESIGN ON GRAPH PAPER BASED ON AROUND 58 ROWS OF WEAVING. IF YOU OPT FOR THIS SIMPLER APPROACH, YOU WILL NEED TO CUT THE BYE-STAKES THE HEIGHT OF THE FINISHED BASKET AND THEY SHOULD BE INSERTED TO THE RIGHT OF EVERY STAKE.

1 For the base, cut 8 x 30 cm (12 in) sticks from No 14 cane. Make a 4-through-4 slath. Using maroon No 5 cane tie in the slath with 2 rows of pairing, open to pairs on the 3rd round and to singles on the 5th round. Continue weaving until the base is 23 cm (9 in) diameter. Stake up with 32 x 76 cm (30 in) stakes cut from No 10 cane.

2 Upsett with 5 rows of 3-rod waling, in the same colour as the base, working a step-up at the end of each row; the stakes should be at a 92-degree angle to the base. Complete the waling. Cut 32 x 51 cm (20 in) bye-stakes from No 10 cane and insert 1 to the right and 1 to the left of every other stake.

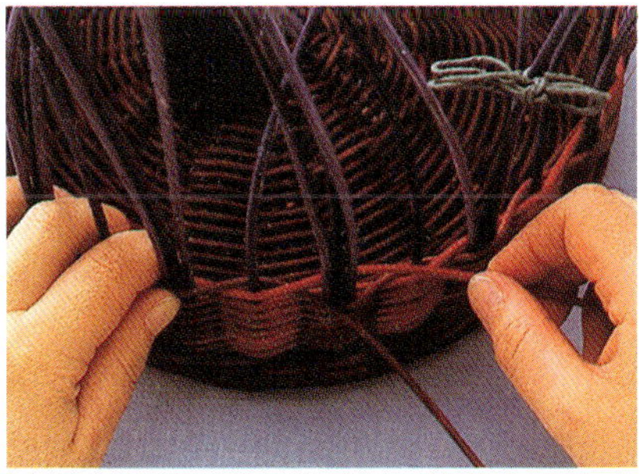

3 Using one of each colour weaver begin pairing. Control the weaving carefully because the irregular positioning of the stakes and bye-stakes can make the weaving slightly "ridged". Pair for 8 rows.

4 Continue pairing, but change the positioning of the stakes and bye-stakes – the singles will become the central stake of a group of 3 and vice versa. To make the 1st row of this procedure easier, pull the outer stakes of the groups of 3 firmly apart, towards the single stake they will be joining. And, when pairing between the new groupings, take the weaver in front of 1 (or 3) pulling it down firmly at the back before taking it behind the next stake, or stakes, and out to the front. ▶

MATERIALS AND EQUIPMENT YOU WILL NEED

SIDE CUTTERS • TAPE MEASURE • NO 14 CANE, DYED PURPLE, FOR THE STICKS • BODKIN • NO 5 CANE, DYED MAROON AND PINK, FOR THE WEAVERS • NO 10 CANE, DYED PURPLE, FOR THE STAKES AND BYE-STAKES • ROUND-NOSED PLIERS • WEIGHT • STRING • 97 CM (38 IN) 10 MM HANDLE CANE, DYED PURPLE • CRAFT KNIFE

5 After 8 rows, return the stakes and bye-stakes to their previous positions, paying particular attention to the 1st row as described in step 4. Control the shape constantly to maintain the cylindrical shape of the basket.

6 Using the side cutters, trim off the ends of joins on the inside of the basket as you work up, otherwise it becomes very difficult to reach them.

7 Work a total of 58 rows (7 blocks of pattern change), and complete pairing. Lay in 3 maroon weavers and work rows of 3-rod waling. Complete waling. Trim off all the bye-stakes, leaving the centre stakes intact. Check the height is level all round.

8 Shave 1 end of the border core (see Shopping Basket). Work the first stage of a 4-rod border by bringing down 4 stakes behind 1. Tie the shaved end of the core to the basket through the waling – it will lie on top of the border stakes that have been brought down. Continue working a 4-rod border over the core (see Shopping Basket).

9 When you are nearing the shaved end of the border core, trim and shave down the other end so that the 2 cut edges will join up to lie neatly side by side. Complete the border (see Shopping Basket).

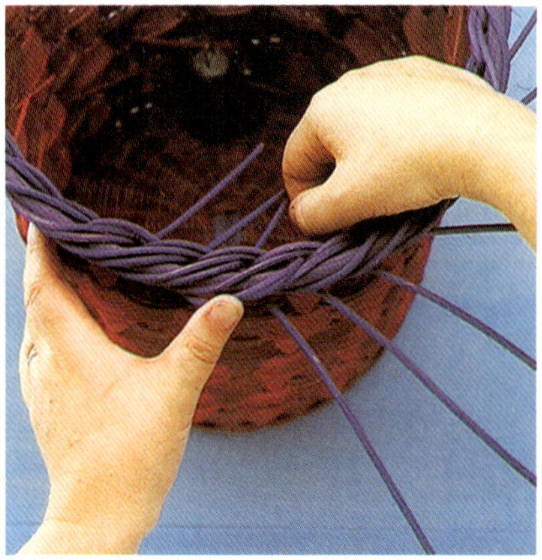

10 Finally, take all the stakes to the inside by bringing each one up over the core again and threading it down between the core and the two strands immediately behind the core. Trim off the ends of all the border stakes so that they lie over a stake.

LIDDED WORK BASKET

IF YOU WISH TO USE THIS BASKET AS A SEWING BASKET, LINE IT WITH FABRIC, OTHERWISE SMALL ITEMS, SUCH AS NEEDLES AND PINS, COULD GET TRAPPED IN THE WEAVING. THIS WOULD ALSO MAKE AN EXCELLENT CONTAINER FOR COSMETICS OR HAIR ACCESSORIES IN THE BEDROOM.

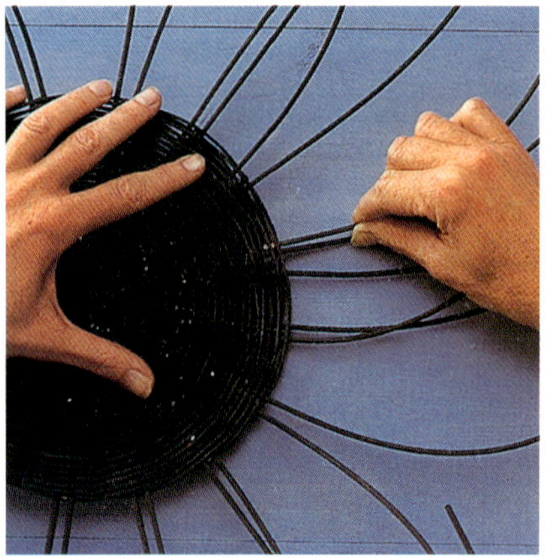

1 Cut 8 x 28 cm (11 in) base sticks from black No 14 cane and make a 4-through-4 slath. Using black No 3 cane, tie in the slath with 2 rows of pairing, opening on the 3rd row into singles. Continue weaving until the base is 21.5 cm (8½ in) diameter. Cut 33 stakes from black No 8 cane, 46 cm (18 in) long and stake up the base. Insert the extra stake wherever there is a wider gap to give a number of stakes divisible by 3. Soak the base well, turn it convex side up, pinch up the stakes and tie above the slath.

2 With the base on its side, begin upsetting with a 4-rod wale in No 6 cane. Mark the step-up.

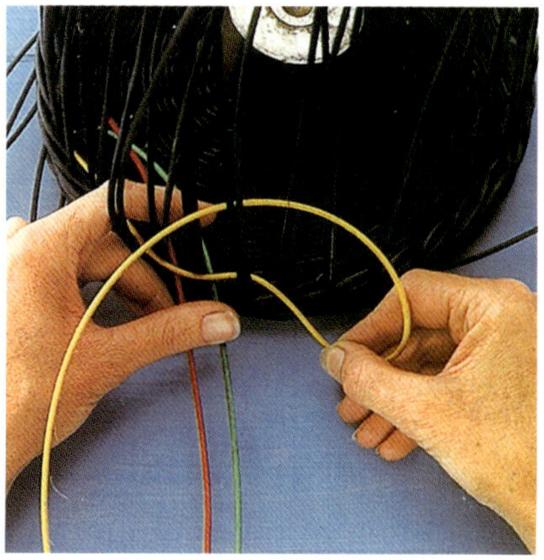

3 Cut 33 bye-stakes from black No 8 cane, 40 cm (16 in) long. Insert 1 to the right of each stake. Begin a 3-rod wale using red, yellow and green No 5 weavers. Begin slightly away from the start of the 4-rod wale. Work 4 complete rows, but with no step-up.

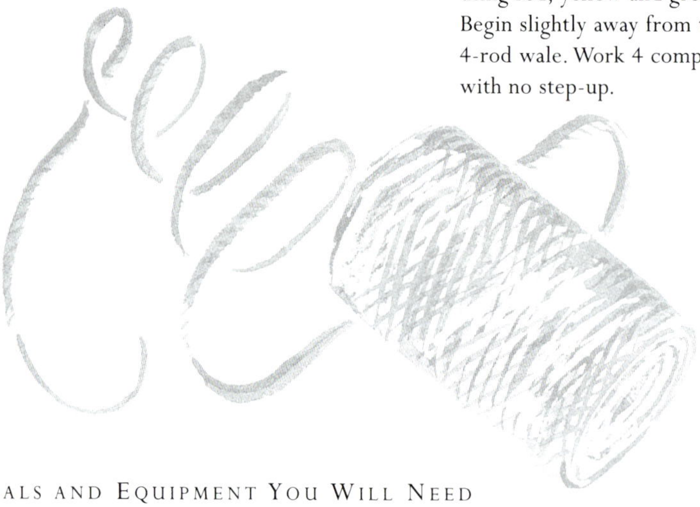

MATERIALS AND EQUIPMENT YOU WILL NEED

SIDE CUTTERS • TAPE MEASURE • BODKIN • NO 14 CANE, DYED BLACK, FOR THE STICK • NO 3 CANE, DYED BLACK, FOR THE BASE WEAVERS • NO 8 CANE, DYED BLACK, FOR THE STAKES, BYE-STAKES AND LID STICKS • CRAFT KNIFE • ROUND-NOSED PLIERS • STRING • NO 6 CANE, DYED BLACK, FOR BOTTOM AND TOP WALE • WEIGHT • NO 5 CANE, DYED RED, YELLOW AND GREEN, FOR THE WEAVERS • NO 3 CANE, DYED BLACK, RED, YELLOW AND GREEN, FOR THE LID WEAVERS • PEGS (OPTIONAL) • 6 CM (2½ IN) X 1 CM (½ IN) HANDLE CANE • BLACK DYE • SECATEURS (SHEARS) • VARNISH AND BRUSH

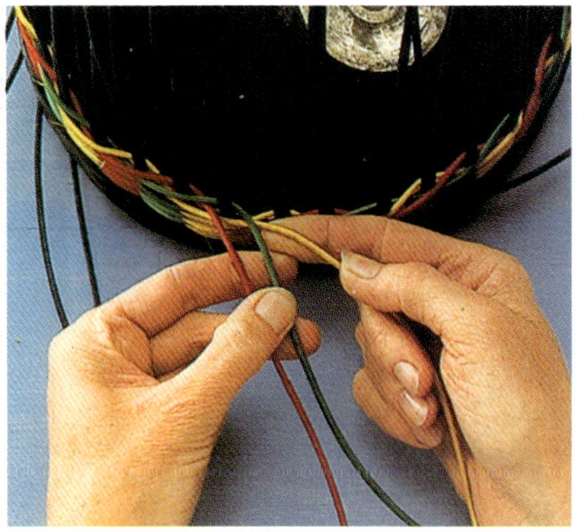

4 Begin working a reverse wale: the left-hand weaver goes *under* the 2 weavers to the right instead of *over* them. (You will work 4 rows, then change back again to weave 4 further rows of ordinary 3-rod wale. Leave the ends on the outside without completing).

5 Joining for reverse waling is done opposite to an ordinary wale. Insert the new weaver when the old weaver is on the inside of the basket and on the right of the 3 weavers. Insert the new weaver so the new end is on the outside of the basket, take the new weaver back out to the front, passing behind the right-hand stake. After the 4 rows of ordinary 3-rod wale, soak the stakes well and pinch them level with the weave, using the round-nosed pliers. Start a 4-rod in front 2, behind 2 wale, having marked the step-up.

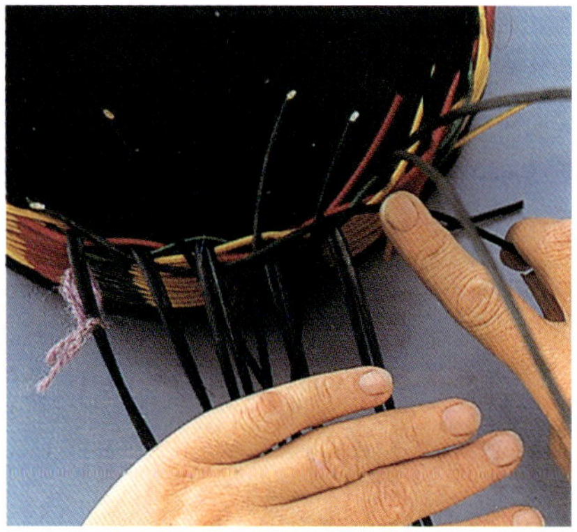

6 Hold the stakes out almost at right angles to the siding as you weave over them. Weave 3 complete rounds then complete. At this stage, there should be a pronounced outward flow to the rim.

7 Start a trac border. Re-soak the stakes if necessary. To help keep spaces of the right height open for the finish of the trac border, insert 3 pairs of No 8 cane scraps about 10 cm (4 in) long between 3 sets of stakes. Treating each pair of stakes as 1 and starting with the pair immediately on top of the dummy spacers, weave in front of 1, behind 1, in front of 1 and behind 1, finishing on the outside of the basket. Do not twist the stakes when weaving.

8 To finish the trac border, remove the dummy spacers and weave each pair of stakes away in strict sequence, each set laying down immediately over the previous set. The last pair will be quite tight. Aim to get the height of the top of the trac border totally level. Trim off.

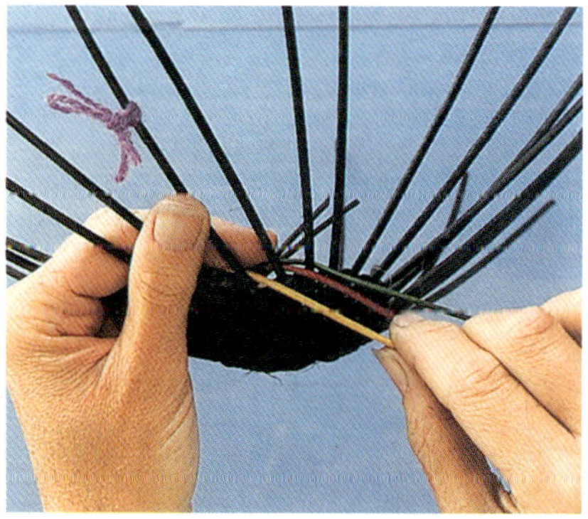

9 For the lid cut 12 x 30 cm (12 in) sticks from black No 8 cane. and make a 6-through-6 slath. Using black No 3 cane, tie in the slath with 2 rows of pairing. Open out into pairs on the 3rd row, then into singles on the 6th. Work 3 rows over singles, aiming for a conical shape. Start a 3-rod wale with red, yellow and green No 3 cane weavers. Change to reverse wale for 3 more rounds. Continue until you have completed 3 blocks of waling and 2 of reverse waling, ending with ordinary waling.

▶

10 Use simple joins as used for randing so that all ends are underneath. Don't worry if they appear slightly loose as the next row of weaving will hold the join tightly in place.

11 Change to 2 black No 3 weavers and pair for 5 rows. Lay in 1 more weaver and work 3 rows of 3-rod waling. Allowing 1.5 cm (¾ in) for the border, check that the lid will be the right size. Add another round of waling if necessary (or remove 1 if it is too big).

12 Leave the ends on the inside, pegging them if necessary. Trim off the sticks level with the weaving.

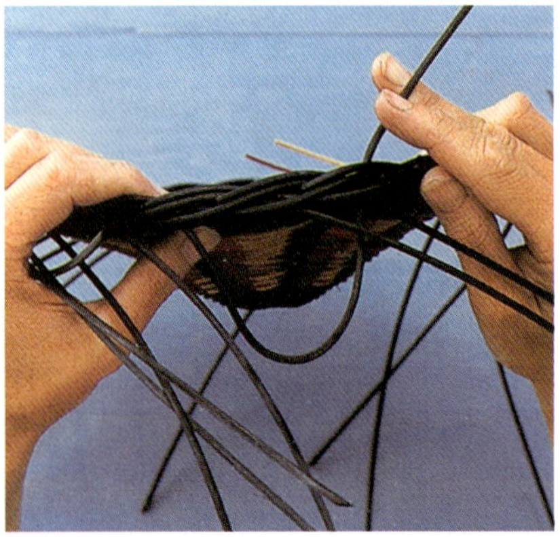

13 Cut 24 x 25 cm (10 in) stakes from black No 8 cane. Turn the lid concave side up and insert a stake to the right of each stick at least 5 cm (2 in) into the weave. Soak the stakes well. Pinch the stakes down. With the right side of the lid towards you, work a 3-rod border. Then work a simple follow-on border. Trim off.

14 Prepare the handle toggle. Cut the ends of the handle cane at an angle with secateurs (shears). Using a craft knife, cut 3 small notches in the centre, 2 mm (1/16 in) apart and deep enough to accommodate No 3 cane. Dye black following the manufacturer's instructions.

15 Soak the centre of the lid well. Taking 1 piece each of well-soaked red, yellow and green No 3 cane, use a bodkin to pierce through the centre of the slath. Thread yellow cane over the toggle and through each hole in the slath. Making sure the cane nestles in the central notch, pull the cane through tightly on the underside and tie with a tight reef knot. Repeat with the other 2 colours in the remaining notches. Trim off the ends carefully, then varnish.

WASHING BASKET

THIS USEFUL, GENERAL PURPOSE BASKET IS IDEAL FOR A SMALL BATHROOM OR BEDROOM. HANDLES CAN BE ADDED, IF YOU WISH: TWISTED WILLOW RODS, ROPE OR STRIPS OF LEATHER THREADED THROUGH THE LID OR EVEN UNDER THE BORDER WOULD ALL WORK WELL. LINSEED OIL, DILUTED WITH 5 PARTS OF WHITE SPIRIT (TURPENTINE) CAN BE APPLIED TO ENHANCE THE FINISHED BASKET. BRUSH IT ON LIGHTLY AND ALLOW TO DRY IN A WELL-VENTILATED ROOM.

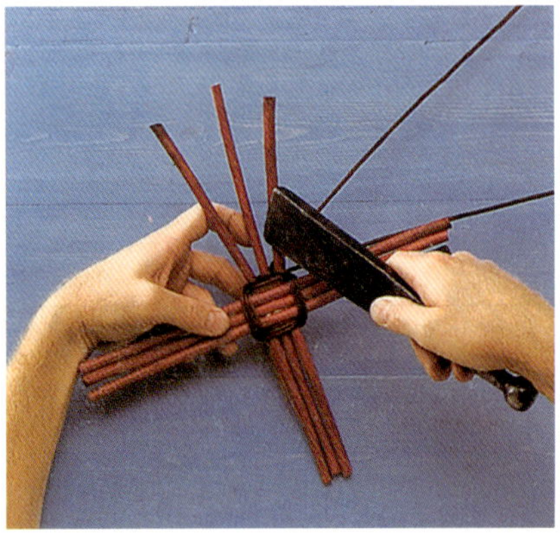

1 Cut 6 x 33 cm (13 in) sticks from willow butts and make a 3-through-3 slath. Arrange the sticks so that they are saucer shaped. You will be weaving the base with the bottom facing you. Thread the tips of 2 fine 90–120 cm (3–4 ft) rods through the left side of the 3 vertical sticks. Take a rod to the right, behind the 3 sticks and bring it to the front. Tie in the slath with pairing for 3 rows, keeping the weaving rods under tension. On the 4th row, open out the sticks into singles and continue pairing, When you have made 3 strokes to each side, beat down with a rapping iron.

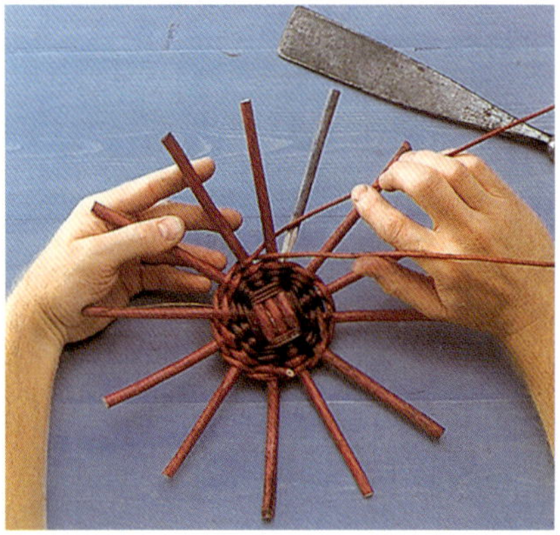

2 Continue weaving out to butts. Join in new rods butt to butt. Weave about 3 strokes beyond the join then slype a 15 cm (6 in) stick (known as a "half-stick") and insert it alongside a base stick. Continue weaving, opening out where the extra stake was added, until the tips are woven in. Now slew the base starting with 1 rod: weave, using randing in front of 1 stake, behind 1 stake. Weave 4 strokes, add another rod, weave round the base, add another rod, weave half round the base, add another rod. Stagger the rods so they are not always inserted in the same place. Join so the butts are always kept on the top surface.

3 Slype the butts of 2 x 1.8 m (6 ft) rods and insert them to the right of 2 consecutive base sticks. Kink the rods about 2 cm (¾ in) above the weaving. Pair around the base to enclose the slewing, continuing until you reach the starting point. Complete pairing.

MATERIALS AND EQUIPMENT YOU WILL NEED

SIDE CUTTERS • TAPE MEASURE • 1.8–2.1 M (6–7 FT) WILLOW RODS, DYED IN 2 COLOURS • BODKIN • 90–120 CM (3–4 FT) WILLOW RODS, DYED IN 2 COLOURS • RAPPING IRON • CRAFT KNIFE • SECATEURS (SHEARS) • 1.5 M (5 FT) WILLOW RODS • GREASE POT • BLUNT KNIFE

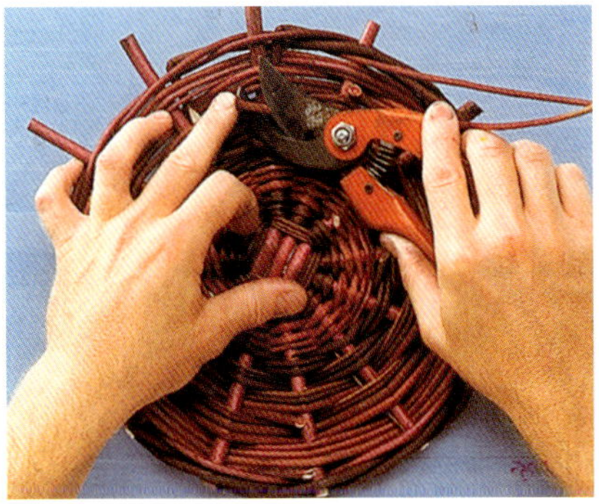

4 Using the secateurs (shears), trim off all the tips and butts. Trim the base sticks level with the edge of the base. Slype 25 x 2.1 m (7 ft) rods. Insert a large greased bodkin alongside a stick, as far up to the centre of the base as possible. Remove the bodkin and insert a stake, with the slyped faces on the bottom, 1 on either side of each stick, except for 1 stick which has only 1 stake. The point should at least touch the pairing near the centre.

5 Stake up the base. Tap the stake 1.5 cm (½ in) into the base using a rapping iron, leaving a 1 cm (¼ in) gap to accommodate the bottom wale.

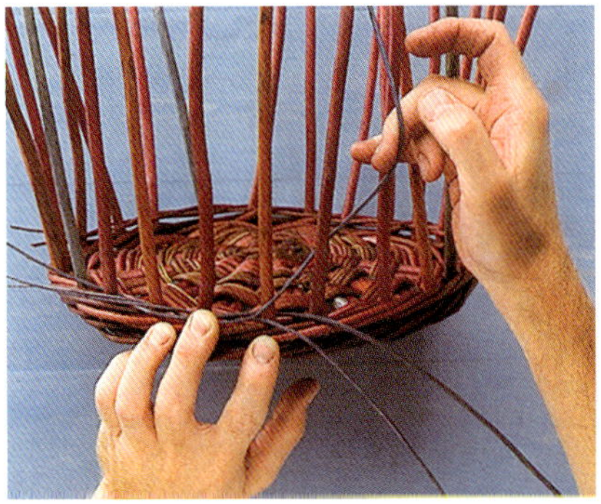

6 Select 8 fine 1.2 m (4 ft) rods. Starting with tips, work a 4-rod upsett with 2 sets of weavers. Trim the bottom of the base and the waling joins, then stand the basket on its base and insert the weight. Rap down.

7 Check the spacing of the stakes is even, re-arranging as necessary. Start slewing using thinner rods, increasing in size as you work up the basket. Place the butt of a small rod on the inside of a stake and weave this rod all the way round. Start another rod about 4 or 5 spaces further on from where the 1st started and weave until you meet the 1st tip. Collect the 2 rods and weave these together until the 1st finishes, leaving the tip on the outside. Add a 3rd rod about 4 or 5 spaces further on from where the1st started and weave round until you meet the 2nd tip. Keep inserting rods to achieve and maintain a 4 or 5 rod thickness. Rap the weaving gently as you go. When you reach 38 cm (15 in), tail off the weaving until the final rod has finished. Rap down level and add a top wale using 6 thin 1.8 m (6 ft) or 6 thick 1.5 m (5 ft) rods.

8 Begin a 6-rod border behind 2 by bringing down 6 stakes behind 2. Leaving a generous curve, place the 1st stake behind the 9th stake and out to the front. Bring down the left-hand upright to make a pair. Continue the 6-rod behind 2 border until only 2 stakes remain upright.

9 Wet the 2 remaining stakes with a sponge and, starting at the border and working towards the tip, draw each one through greased fingers in order to make the willow pliant. Thread each behind 2 stakes and through to the front.

▶

10 Complete the border, threading the right-hand stake of each 6 pairs in the correct sequence to maintain the pattern of the border.

11 For the lid, cut 10 sticks 10 cm (4 in) longer than the outside diameter of the border. Make and tie in a 5-through 5-slath. Complete 2 sets of pairing. Take 20 x 1.5 m (5 ft) rods and insert a tip upwards into each space ready for working a block of French randing. After several rounds, lay the lid on the basket. Check the internal diameter of the basket with the width of the lid. Complete each round of weaving and stop when the lid is 5 mm (¼ in) smaller all round than the inside of the basket.

12 With the wrong side of the lid facing, lift up the ends of the rods vertically against the sticks of the lid and, using the width of the knife blade, bend the rods back over the knife and release. Do this to all 20 rods, ready to form the rim of the lid which will locate inside the basket.

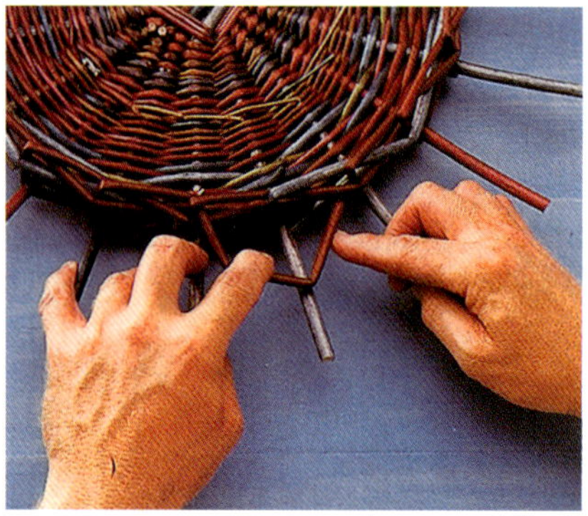

13 Make a trac border with the kinked rods: working left to right, work behind a rod and in front of the next, then behind the next to rest inside the 4th. Trim with secateurs (shears) on the inside, leaving 1.5 cm (½ in) overhanging. Place the last 2 rods along where they will be threaded then kink and trim them before weaving them in.

14 Turn the lid the right way up. Using 6 x 1.5 m (5 ft) rods, work a 3-rod wale, starting with tips, joining butts and finishing with tips. Squeeze the trac border tight and maintain a domed lid. You will need to leave about 1.5 cm (½ in) all round the outside of the lid in order to put on the final border. If you do need an extra wale, start the tips on the opposite side of the lid to balance it out. With the inside of the lid facing you, and using a greased bodkin, insert 20 x 1.5 m (5 ft) rods on the left-hand side of each stick. Work a 3-rod border. Finally, to finish off, trim off all butts on the inside and all tips on the outside.

CANE PLATTER

COMBINING PACKING AND WALING PRODUCES DRAMATIC PATTERNS AND INTERESTING SHAPES. THE PATTERN COULD BE DEVELOPED BY INTRODUCING MORE COLOURS. IT IS IMPORTANT TO KEEP THE STAKES AS EVENLY SPACED AS POSSIBLE THROUGHOUT THE WEAVING OF THE PLATTER.

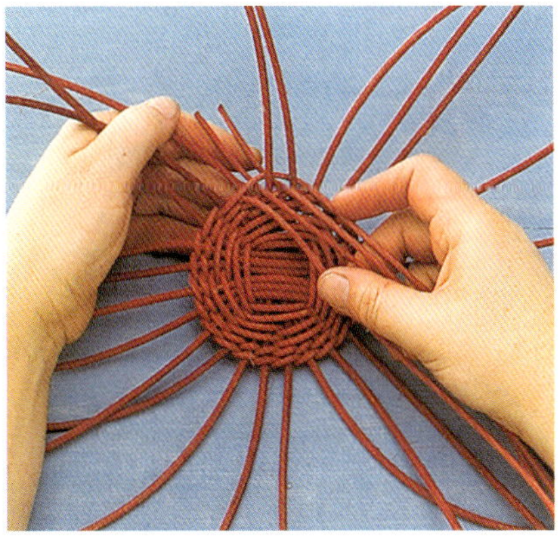

1 Make a 6-through-6 slath with No 10 cane, and tie it in with 2 rows of pairing using No 5 cane. On the 3rd row open the stakes to groups of 3 and on the 5th row open them out to singles. At the beginning of the 7th row lay in 2 additional weavers to the right of the existing 2 weavers, and begin working 1 row of 4-rod wale variation: in front of 2 stakes, behind 2 stakes. This will create a small ridge on the underside of the basket for it to sit on. Complete this row of waling by taking all 4 weavers to the back.

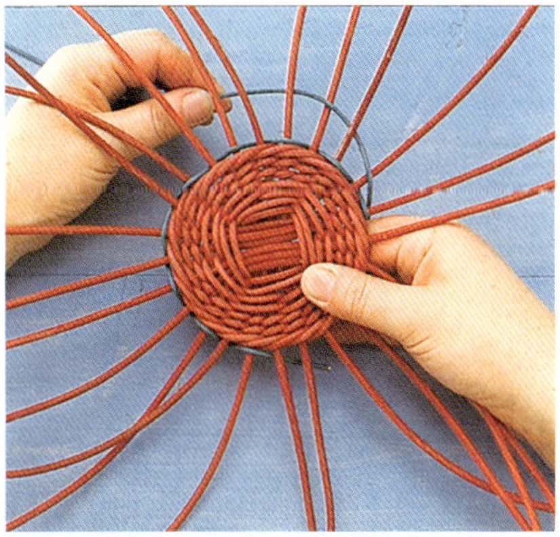

2 Look at the slath and select 1 corner of the square. Mark with small pieces of string the 2 stakes from the slath which are either side of this corner. Including each of these corner stakes count 9 stakes to the left and to the right – 18 stakes in total – and mark the 2 outer stakes. Using a strand of the No 3 cane, pack over these 18 stakes until you have worked round just the 2 marked central stakes, taking great care to keep the stakes evenly spaced. Lay in 3 No 5 cane weavers and work 1 row of 3-rod waling, completing the waling after the step-up.

3 Look at the slath again and mark the 2 stakes on either side of the opposite corner of the slath. Count out from these stakes and mark the 2 outer stakes as before – 18 stakes. Work the 2nd block of packing over these stakes, using a strand of the darker coloured No 3 cane. ▶

MATERIALS AND EQUIPMENT YOU WILL NEED

SIDE CUTTERS • BODKIN OR BRADAWL • NO 10 CANE, DYED, FOR THE STICKS AND STAKES • NO 5 CANE, DYED, FOR THE WEAVERS • STRING • NO 3 CANE, DYED IN TWO SHADES, FOR THE PACKING WEAVERS • PEG • ROUND-NOSED PLIERS • VARNISH AND BRUSH

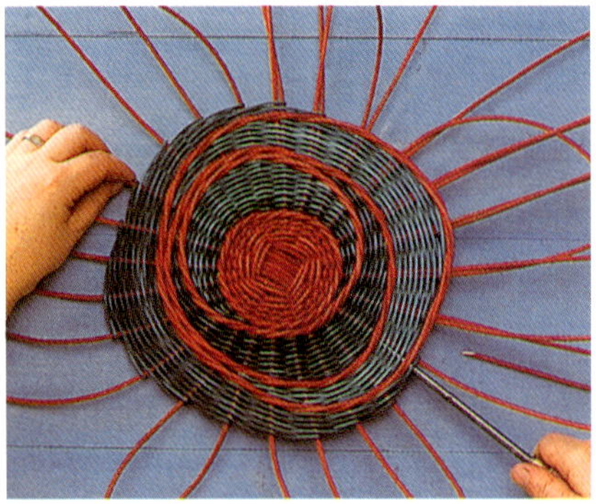

4 Work another round of 3-rod waling with No 5 cane. Then work a 3rd block of packing using the lighter coloured No 3 cane, again over 18 stakes. This time the central 2 stakes of the 18 stakes will be the 2 stakes on either side of one of the 2 remaining corners of the slath. Enclose the packing with a round of 3-rod waling. Next work a 4th block of packing, again over 18 stakes, the central 2 of which will be either side of the 4th corner of the slath. With the right side facing, insert 24 stakes of No 10 cane, 20 cm (8 in) long, to the left of each stake. Push them down as far as the 2nd row of 3-rod waling.

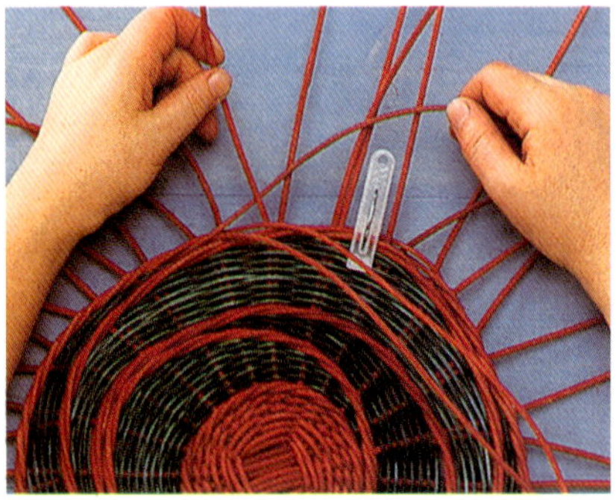

5 Insert 3 No 5 weavers into 3 consecutive spaces, gently pulling apart the pairs of stakes to do this. Peg the 3 weavers in place. Work a row of 3-rod waling, opening up the pairs of stakes to singles.

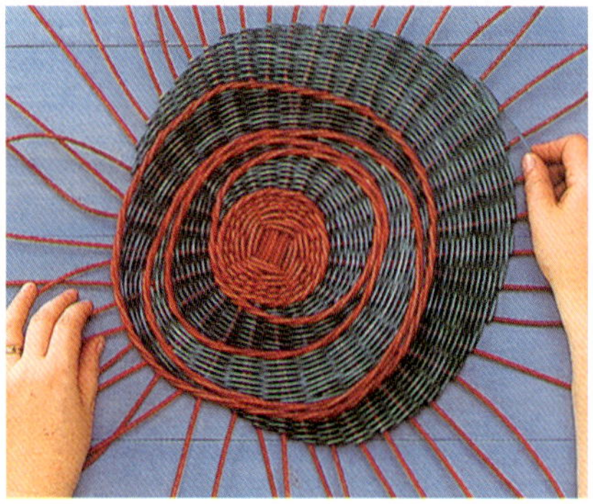

6 Work a 5th block of packing over 36 stakes, the central 2 stakes being located above the central 2 stakes of the 1st block of packing.

7 Enclose the 5th block of packing with 1 row of 3-rod waling. Work a 6th block of packing, again over 36 stakes, the central 2 of which are located above the central 2 stakes of the 2nd block of packing. Enclose this final block of packing with 3 rows of 3-rod waling. Trim the stakes flush with the waling and insert a new 50 cm (20 in) stake to the left of each trimmed one. Push down to previous rows of waling enclosing packing.

8 Soak the stakes then pinch them up at right angles to the platter. Insert a 4th weaver and work 1 row of 4-rod waling holding up the stakes as you weave tightly round them. At the end of the row, take the weavers to the back/outside and continue to weave tightly, working 2 further rows of 4-rod waling; you will be working from right to left for these 2 rows, the change of direction creating a chevron pattern around the outside edge. When these 2 rows are complete, the stakes should be at right angles to the base of the platter. Complete the waling.

9 Work a 4-rod border followed by a 3-rod follow-on border, and varnish.

SUPPLIERS & ACKNOWLEDGEMENTS

AUTHOR'S ACKNOWLEDGEMENTS

Thanks are due to the following people for their contribution:

To the contributors: Hilary Burns, Mary Butcher, John Galloway, Jo Gilmour and Susie Thomson.

To the people who lent baskets for the Gallery: Dail Behennah; Hilary Burns; Mr and Mrs Endersby, who lent the basket they own created by their neice, Alex Bury; Jo Gilmour; Sally Goymer; Mary Butcher, who lent the work she owns by Marian Gwiazda; Geraldine Jones; Susie Thomson, who lent the basket she owns by John Galloway.

To the people who lent baskets for the History section: Mary Butcher and Shuna Rendel.

To the makers of the baskets on pages 6 and 7, Monsieur Coudoin (left-hand basket), Colin Manthorpe (centre basket) and Terry Bensley (right-hand basket)

To the photographers of the steps and final shots, respectively Mark Wood and his assistant Eddie and Peter Williams, and to Georgina Rhodes for her inspired styling.

PUBLISHER'S ACKNOWLEDGEMENTS

Thank you to the following for loaning props for photography:

Evans Cycles, 127-9 Wandsworth High Street, London SW18

Joss Graham, 10 Ecclestone Street, London SW1

Paperchase, 213 Tottenham Court Road, London W1

Young & D, Beckhaven House, 9 Gilbert Road, London SE11

SUPPLIERS

United Kingdom

Jacobs, Young & Westbury
Bridge Road
Haywards Heath
West Sussex RH16 1UA
tel: 01444 412 411
(centre cane, chair cane, selection of basketry tools)

The Cane Workshop
The Gospel Hall
Westport, Langport
Somerset TA10 0BH
tel: 01460 281 636)
(basketry tools and chair cane)

Fred Aldous Ltd
Dept BA
37 Lever Street
Manchester M60 1UX
tel: 0161 236 2477
(centre cane, chair cane, basketry tools)

United States

ACP Inc.,
120 Elmwood Drive
Salisbury, NC 28147
tel: (704) 636 3034

Basket Beginnings
25 Westtioga Street
Tunkhannock, PA 18567
tel: (717) 836 6080

The Caning Shop
926 Gilman Street
Berkeley CA 94710

John McGuire
398 S. Main
Geneva, NY 14456
tel: (315) 781 1251

The Noresta
320B Western Avenue
Allegan, MI 49010
tel: (616) 673 3249

H H Perkins Co.
10 S. Bradley Road
Woodbridge, CT 06525
tel: (203) 389 9501

V I Reed & Cane
Rt. 5, PO Box 632
Rogers, AR 72756
tel: (501) 789 2639

BIBLIOGRAPHY AND FURTHER READING

The list below is by no means exhaustive; further reading lists can be obtained by contacting the addresses listed in Further Information.

The Complete Book of Baskets and Basketry, Dorothy Wright, David & Charles, 1983, UK
Contemporary Wicker Basketry, Flo Hoppe, Lark Books, 1996, USA
Creative Basketmaking, Lois Walpole, Collins & Brown, 1989, UK
Journal of Museum Ethnography, No 4, Polly Pollock, Museum Ethnographers Group, 1994, UK
Modern Basketry Techniques (revised edition), Mary Butcher, BT Batsford, 1989, UK
Start-A-Craft: Basketmaking, Polly Pollock, Apple Press, 1994, UK
The Techniques of Basketry, Virginia Harvey, BT Batsford, UK
Wicker Basketry, Flo Hoppe, Interweave Press, USA
Willow Work, Mary Butcher, Dryad Press, 1986, UK

FURTHER INFORMATION

The Basket-maker's Association
King William Cottage
Yalberton Road
Nr Paignton
Devon TQ4 7PE, UK
(reading lists and information available)

INDEX